God's Perfect Plan

by

Kelly Ellis

ISBN 1-58427-066-7

Guardian of Truth Foundation
P.O. Box 9670
Bowling Green, Kentucky 42102

Introduction

A rapid move to a low appreciation of the Divine Plan of the ages to redeem fallen mån is manifest in so many ways that it needs no proof to the discerning Christian. Many, whose work in the Lord covers many years of faithful service, are aware of this trend and have expressed hope that someone might perform the task of giving us materials to assist us in understanding God's love and concern for us.

Brother Kelly Ellis has, with some encouragement, produced this work. Brother Ellis has been for nearly forty years engaged in the educational system of Kentucky and labored during this time as an evangelist also. He is eminently qualified for the work herein. His work has proven him to be both capable and safe as a teacher of the word of God.

We are glad to offer this work of twenty-six lessons to brethren everywhere. We believe this work will get results. We encourage churches to use it regularly in the Bible study work. It will offer much to all who do personal evangelism. It will not only offer one a guide in study, but will give the materials necessary to convert a sinner and ground him scripturally in the eternal purpose of God.

—*Earl E. Robertson*

Table of Contents

Chapter One

Chapter Two

Chapter Three

Chapter Four

Chapter Five

CHAPTER I

Lesson I: Introduction

Text

"For this cause I Paul, the prisoner of Jesus Christ for you Gentiles, If ye have heard of the dispensation of the grace of God which is given me to you-ward: How that by revelation he made known unto me the mystery; (as I wrote afore in few words, whereby, when ye read, ye may understand my knowledge in the mystery of Christ) which in other ages was not made known unto the sons of men, as it is now revealed unto his holy apostles and prophets by the Spirit; That the Gentiles should be fellowheirs, and of the same body, and partakers of his promise in Christ by the gospel: Whereof I was made a minister, according to the gift of the grace of God given unto me by the effectual working of his power. Unto me, who am less than the least of all saints, is this grace given, that I should preach among the Gentiles the unsearchable riches of Christ; And to make all men see what is the mystery, which from the beginning of the world hath been hid in God, who created all things by Jesus Christ; To the intent that now unto the principalities and powers in heavenly places might be known by the church the manifold wisdom of God, According to the eternal purpose which he purposed in Christ Jesus our Lord" (Eph. 3:1-11).

Commentary

The text is a complete and comprehensive statement of the eternal purpose of God in human redemption. The gospel of Christ, the seed of the kingdom, and the church which results from the sowing of that seed into good and honest hearts, constitute the eternal plan of God for the salvation of mankind.

The scheme of redemption did not come into existence accidentally and unplanned. The church did not originate as the result of political revolution and conquest (John 18:36); it is not a social institution, the outgrowth of first-century culture; it was not designed to meet the social needs of man, and it does not depend for its continued existence upon the proclamation of a social gospel. The spiritual body of Christ did not begin as a benevolent organization in the midst of economic depression, nor as an arrangement to provide entertainment and recreation for the physical enjoyment and development of its members.

The church of Jesus Christ is a spiritual relationship between God and man, the end result of the purpose of God for
the spiritual welfare of all men who will conform to His
requirements. As members of it, mortal men can enjoy all of
the spiritual blessings which God provides in this life and en-
tertain the hope of eternal life in the world to come.

A careful reading of the text will show that this perfect
plan was a Godhead arrangement:

(1) God planned it before the worlds were created.

(2) Jesus Christ procured it by His death upon the cross.

(3) The Holy Spirit has revealed it through inspired men.

The careful reader will also observe that there are three
provisions included in this plan:

(1) The coming of the Son of God to be the Savior of the
world in keeping with all of the Old Testament promises and
prophecies concerning Him. God's eternal purpose was in
Christ (v. 11).

(2) The revelation of the mystery of the gospel by the Holy
Spirit (vs. 2-6).

(3) The church as the spiritual institution which reflects
the widsom of God and through which men can ascribe glory to
Him in this life (v. 10; Eph. 3:21).

This three-fold arrangement represents everything which
the grace of God has provided for man's redemption:

(1) The death of Christ was a demonstration of the love and
the grace of God (Heb. 2:9).

(2) The revelation of the mystery was accomplished
through a dispensation of Divine Grace (vs. 2-6).

(3) The "exceeding riches of his grace" is reflected by the
church throughout the ages (Eph. 2:6-8).

Although salvation by the grace of God as outlined in the
plan above, existed as a concept in the mind of God before man
was created, it does not exclude faith and obedience on the part
of man; nor does it teach that men were predestinated apart
from their will and choice in the matter. It was the *plan* that
was foreordained, not the individual. Men are saved by grace
through faith in that plan (Eph. 2:8).

The Calvinistic concept of the predestination of men apart

from their will and choice, issues from the false assumption that men "are born in sin," having inherited the original sin of Adam, and "being wholly inclined to evil," with no good in them, such a condition required an "unconditional election" on the part of God. This election limited the atonement of Christ to the "elect," who are saved eternally by the "irresistible grace of God," and will, therefore, never be able to forfeit their right to eternal life. On the other hand, all who are not of the "elect" are completely shut off from the grace of God which He has extended to all men through Christ, and are eternally consigned to damnation and separation from God in the world to come.

Both revelation and reason rebel against the false doctrine of predestination. It stands opposed to New Testament teaching on at least five points.

1. It makes God a respecter of persons in that He has predestinated some to eternal life and others to eternal damnation; this is contrary to the very nature of God (Rom. 2:11; Deut. 32:4).

2. It makes God responsible for the loss of souls in hell; but the New Testament teaches that He is not "willing that any should perish, but that all should come to repentance" (2 Pet. 3:9). He "would have all men to be saved" (1 Tim. 2:4).

3. It destroys man's power of choice. If my destiny is already sealed, there is nothing I can do to change it; I have no choice open to me, and my will cannot be exercised in any way whatever. However, the Bible says, "Choose you this day whom ye will serve" (Josh. 24:15), and the "Spirit and the bride say, Come . . . . And whosoever *will*, let him take the water of life freely" (Rev. 22:17). Jesus said, "If any man *will*" (Jn. 7:17).

4. It nullifies the commission of Christ (Mk. 16:15-16). If one's eternal destiny has already been determined by the Father, why preach the gospel to him?

5. The whole system makes man an irresponsible being. If man is born in sin, if he is a sinner by birth, he is not responsible for those transgressions; but man does not *inherit* sin—he *commits* it (Ezek. 18:1-24). The passage also teaches that man

does not inherit righteousness; he does it. God has created man upright; he becomes evil when he "seeks" to be evil (Ecc. 7:29). The "equality of God's way" provides for the unrighteous man to be made righteous, and for the righteous to be made unrighteous. Man decides his relationship to God in the present life, and thus determines his destiny by the exercise of his own will (Ezek. 18:25-28).

Questions

1. God purposed man's redemption before the creation; does this make God responsible for Adam's sin? _____.

2. Explain: _____
_____
_____

3. What is the difference between foreknowledge and foreordination? _____
_____
_____

4. Christians are *elect* according to the *foreknowledge* of God (1 Pet. 1:1-2). Explain: _____
_____
_____

5. The Thessalonians had, "from the beginning," been chosen (elected) to salvation (2 Thess. 2:13-14). How and when?
_____
_____

6. How are men called of God? _____
_____

7. Jesus said that one must become as a little child in order to enter the kingdom of heaven (Matt. 18:3). Show how this statement refutes the idea of "total depravity." _____
_____
_____

8. Give some passages to show that man determines his own destiny. _____
_____
_____
_____

9. Does the passage in Rom. 9:10-13 teach the predestination of the soul of man? _____ Explain. _____

_____

_____

_____

10. When was the statement in Rom. 9:12 fulfilled? _____
_____ (2 Sam. 8:14).

11. Study Rom. 16:25-26 and answer the following questions:

a. Paul said that the revelation of the "mystery, the eternal purpose of God, was according _____and the _____

_____

b. In what respect was it "by the scriptures of the prophets"?

_____

c. Why has it been made known? _____

_____

Lesson II: God's Plan And Grace

Text

"Who hath saved us, and called us with an holy calling, not according to our works, but according to his own purpose and grace, which was given us in Christ Jesus before the world began" (2 Tim. 1:9).

Commentary

In this verse the apostle restates what he had written in the text of Lesson I. Salvation for "the called of God" is not "according to our works," but according to the purpose of God which He purposed in Christ "before the world began." The apostle declares further that the purpose of God was the product of His grace.

Salvation in Christ cannot be obtained by some system of works devised by the wisdom of men (Tit. 3:5). Neither can that salvation be enjoyed as a result of man's perfect obedience to the commands which are set forth in that plan. However, the grace of God makes provision for the sins of the Christian, even as it provides for the remission of sins of the alien. The grace of God is conditional: "For by grace are ye saved through faith; and that not of yourselves; it is the gift of God" (Eph. 2:8). Justification by the grace of God demands faith on the part of man. We shall see in the next lesson that the faith of Eph. 2:8 is an "obedient faith."

Since some of the false concepts of sin and grace, as taught by Calvin, are currently being accepted and taught by some of the brethren, it is essential to make the following observations:

(1) Although the Christian can never live a "sinlessly perfect life," this does not mean that he is guaranteed unconditional forgiveness of his sins. The Christian will sin from time to time, but those sins will be forgiven through the advocacy of Christ only when he meets the conditions prescribed by the grace of God (1 John 1:7-9; 2:1-2; Acts 8:22).

(2) The grace of God does not cover the sins of ignorance and human weakness unconditionally. If a Christian sins once, he is a sinner, and must seek forgiveness on God's terms (Lev. 10:1-3; Jas. 2:10; Acts 8:18-23).

(3) The grace of God does not allow for the unconditional pardon of sins which the Christian "intended" to make right, but somehow never got around to correcting. New Testament Christianity is not the "religion of intent;" it is the religion of doing what Jesus commanded (Matt. 7:21; Lk. 6:46; 1 John 1:9; Acts 8:22).

(4) God does not impute the personal righteousness (perfect obedience) of Christ to the Christian in place of his unrighteousness (imperfect obedience). The righteousness of the righteous is counted for him, and the wickedness of the wicked is counted against him. However, the wicked man can turn from his wickedness and "do that which is lawful and right," in which case he will be made righteous. This is an unchangeable principle. Just as in the examples of Abraham and David, the Christian's sins will be counted to him until he meets the conditions upon which God has promised forgiveness; when he meets those conditions, his faith (obedient faith) is counted to him for righteousness (Rom. 4:23-25; Psa. 32:1-5; 1 John 1:7-9).

(5) The grace of God does not provide for an "all-incompassing" fellowship with "brethren in error" (Christian Church, Institutionalism, Premillenialism, etc.). Men are called into fellowship with Christ by obedience to the gospel (1 Cor. 1:9; 2 Thess. 2:13-14). Men stay in fellowship with Christ by obedience.

That man is saved by grace, is too plainly taught in the New Testament to require any further argument as to the fact of it. Salvation by the grace of God is clearly taught in such passages as Eph. 2:8-9; 1 Cor. 15:10; Tit. 2:11-12; Rom. 3:24; Rom. 5:20; and many others that might be referred to. However, just *how* men are saved by grace is quite another matter. It is essential, then, that we look at grace as it is related to the purpose and plan of God.

Perhaps the best passage in the New Testament setting forth the relationship between God's grace and man's redemption is Eph. 2:8: "For by grace are ye saved through faith; and that not of yourselves; it is the gift of God." The passage teaches that there are two sides involved in the scheme for man's redemption—the Divine and the human—God's part and man's part. Grace expresses God's part, and faith expresses man's part. Man is not saved by grace alone; this would exclude faith upon the part of man and make him simply a passive recipient of Jehovah's favor. And since God is no respector of persons (Rom. 2:11), all men would then be saved by the favor of God. Universal salvation is the inevitable result of the doctrine of salvation by grace alone. God offers salvation to all men, but all men do not meet the conditions of that system of grace revealed in the gospel of Christ.

The text of Eph. 2:8 teaches that salvation by the grace of God demands faith upon the part of man. One cannot find in the entire Bible a single example of deliverance by the grace of God where faith is not required of men in order to lay hold upon the salvation which the Lord offered. Study the examples of this principle which are cited in the passages given.

1. The salvation of Noah and his family in the ark was a matter of grace (Gen. 6:8), but Noah was saved by faith in the command of God (Heb. 11:7).

2. When the Israelites crossed the Red Sea, God gave Moses a plan for the crossing—God's grace intervened, and the people were admonished to "stand still and see the salvation of the Lord" that day (Ex. 14:13). However, it was by faith that "they crossed the Red Sea as by dry land" (Heb. 11:29).

3. God's grace devised a means by which the children of Israel could be healed from snakebite which had come about as a result of their rebellion against Him; but He required faith that would move them to "look and live" (Num. 21:4-9).

4. Jesus reminded Nicodemus of the above incident as being typical of His being lifted up on the cross; the cross of Christ was an expression of God's love and grace (Heb. 2:9). But Jesus also told Nicodemus that faith in Him as the Son of God was the primary condition of salvation in Christ (John 3:14-16).

5. God's grace provided a plan for the armies of Israel under the leadership of Joshua to capture the city of Jericho (Josh. 6:1-5), but it was "by faith" that the walls of Jericho fell (Heb. 11:30).

6. After God by His grace had saved "the people out of the land of Egypt," He later "destroyed them that believed not" (Jude 3). When man abandons his faith, he forfeits his access to the grace of God. The passage clearly teaches that a believer can become an unbeliever.

Conclusion

In all of the examples given above, men found themselves in situations from which they could not free themselves by their own wisdom and power; only the grace and power of Jehovah could provide salvation. It is clearly evident, however, that such deliverance was not by grace alone; in every case faith was required of the people who were saved by God's grace. All of these examples were written for our instruction (Rom. 15:4); they are examples of salvation by grace through faith as stated in Eph. 2:8. Paul declared that salvation in Christ is offered to men under the gospel on the same principle as exemplified by these Old Testament references. It is by faith that men have "access" to the grace of God in Christ (Rom. 1:1-2). In the next lesson we shall examine the kind of faith which the gospel of Christ requires for men to be "saved by grace through faith."

Questions

1. Define *Grace*. _____

2. Define *Faith*. _____

3. Why did Noah find grace in the eyes of God? _____

_____

4. The Hebrew writer says that when Noah prepared an ark for the salvation of his family, he "condemned the world." Explain. _____

_____

5. The salvation of eight souls in the ark was a "type" or "figure" of _____

_____(1 Pet. 3:21).

6. In the New Testament the crossing of the Red Sea is referred to as a _____(1 Cor. 10:1-2). Explain how it can be described as such. _____

_____

7. Explain how the walls of Jericho fell down "by faith." __
_____

8. Read the entire 6th chapter of Genesis and tell how the faith of Noah enabled him to be saved by grace. _____
_____
_____(Give the passage.)

9. What does Jude 3 and 1 Cor. 10 teach concerning the possibility of "falling from grace"? _____
_____

10. Why were these examples called to our attention? ____
_____(Passage.)

Lesson III: God's Plan And Faith

Text

"Ye see then how that by works a man is justified, and not by faith only" (Jas. 2:24).

Commentary

The text above is the only place in the New Testament where the expression, "by faith only," is found and, in this text, James says that it is not true. James had been discussing the faith of Abraham as demonstrated in the offering of Isaac and declared that he was justified by works in so doing. He further affirmed that the Scripture "which saith, Abraham believed God, and it was imputed unto him for righteousness...," was not fulfilled until his faith had been made complete through his obedience to the command of Jehovah. Abraham proved himself to be a believer, and was accepted of God as a righteous man and a Friend, "not by faith only," but by his works. Had Abraham not been willing to do all that God commanded, James implied that his faith would have been dead—as dead as is the body without the spirit (v. 26).

As a result of Abraham's obedience, he was called "the Friend of God." God's "Friend" is the individual who obeys Him (Jn. 15:14). The faith that saves is the faith that obeys; it is the "faith which worketh by love" (Gal. 5:6). Saving faith is that faith which, when motivated by love for God and for His truth, will move one to render complete obedience to all that God demands of him.

The doctrine of justification by faith only was first advanced by Martin Luther. In his effort to divorce himself from the undue emphasis which the Catholic church placed upon works, he moved to the opposite extreme and propagated the faith only theory. Believing that Paul taught salvation by "faith only" in such passages as Rom. 3:28, and finding James teaching salvation by works as an expression of faith, he concluded that James disagreed with Paul. He, therefore, rejected

the epistle of James as not being entitled to a place in the
Sacred Scriptures.

Any man who interprets the New Testament so as to make
James contradict Paul, disregards one of the elementary rules
of Bible study: the consideration of the context—the subject or
principle being discussed and the purpose of it. When one ap-
plies this rule in comparing Paul's letter to the church at Rome
with the letter written by James, one will readily see that
there is no disagreement.

In the Roman letter, Paul pressed the proposition of Rom.
1:16 that the gospel of Christ is the power of God to save men
in this dispensation, not the law of Moses; and that law had
been done away in Christ. He argued that no flesh, Jew or Gentile, can be justified by the deeds of the law (Rom. 3:20).
Justification, he said, is by faith in the blood of Christ and it is
without the deeds of the law (Rom. 3:20-28). Paul further
stated that God promised Abraham that He would bless all
nations in his seed (Christ). But if one is justified by the works
of the law, that promise is made of no effect, and faith in Jesus
Christ is empty and vain.

On the other hand, James refers to Abraham as being
justified by works before the law of Moses was ever given; but
his justification was by works as a proof of his faith in God.
Paul wrote of the works of the law which make faith *void* (4:14)
while James talked about works of obedience which make faith
perfect (2:22).

When James said that faith without works is dead, he was
simply saying that faith must be demonstrated in acts of
obedience. Before a thing can be done "by faith," God must
have spoken concerning that thing; for faith comes by hearing
the word of God (Rom. 10:17). When God speaks, men are
obligated to give heed, to obey all that He commands (Heb.
2:1-4). Jesus taught that one should not profess faith in Him as
Lord unless that one is willing to do what He commands him to
do (Lk. 6:46; Matt. 7:21).

Perhaps the one chapter in the New Testament which best
explains what it means to do a thing "by faith," is the 11th
chapter of the Hebrew epistle. In this chapter the apostle gives

a long list of Old Testament characters who were justified by faith. He showed clearly that in every instance their faith motivated them to obey God's instructions to the letter.

Questions

1. According to Jesus, who can enter the kingdom of heaven?_____

_____(passage).

2. Define *faith:* _____

_____

3. What is the source of this "evidence"? _____

_____

4. Why was Abel's sacrifice "more excellent" than Cain's?

_____

5. How do we know that God instructed Cain and Abel as to the kind of sacrifice He desired?_____

_____

6. Upon what basis did God translate Enoch "that he should not see death"? _____

_____

7. Having been warned of God concerning the coming flood, Noah demonstrated his faith when he _____

_____

8. Give three examples of the faith of Abraham as set forth in the 11th chapter of Hebrews: _____

_____

_____

9. How did Abraham prove his faith in each case? _____

_____

10. What choice did Moses make "by faith"? _____

_____

11. Why did Moses make that choice? _____

_____

12. Name some Old Testament worthies whose faith is not described in detail in Hebrews 11. _____

_____

13. Choose one of these and show how that individual was justified by faith: _____

_____

14. What is the promise of Heb. 11:39? _____

15. What is the "better thing" of Heb. 11:40? _____

Lesson IV: God's Plan And Eternal Life
Text
"In hope of eternal life, which God, that cannot lie, promised before the world began" (Tit. 1:2).

Commentary

The passage clearly connects the promise and hope of eternal life with the eternal purpose of God. God promised it "before the world began," and Paul was serving God "according to the faith," and in keeping with "the truth which is after godliness." Thus Paul served the Lord as one "in hope of eternal life."

The ultimate end of God's purpose is eternal life with the Father in heaven. Both the Old and New Testaments teach that this present life is but a period of preparation for the world to come. The Bible teaches, therefore, that the whole purpose of this earthly sojourn is to make that preparation.

Solomon declared that the real issue of life is to fear Jehovah and do His will (Ecc. 12:13-14). This is the supreme purpose of every human life. Paul said, "For to me to live is Christ, and to die is gain" (Phil. 1:21). Thus, inspiration teaches that men are to live in this life in a way that will make it possible for them, after death, to live eternally with the Father.

In opposition to this principle, Calvinism teaches that Christians have eternal life as a present possession, and that they can never be lost no matter what or how many sins they commit. This doctrine of "once in grace, always in grace," says that the child of God has eternal life now, and since it is eternal, it will never be possible for him to sin so as to be lost. What does the New Testament teach on the matter? If Jesus did not teach it, it is not true.

The Spirit of Man Is Eternal

Every individual has within him the breathed-in nature of his Creator (Gen. 2:7). God formed the spirit of man within him (Zech. 12:1). That spirit will never die in the sense of ceasing to exist. It will ultimately live with God forever (Matt. 25:34, 46),

17

or it will suffer the torments of hell eternally (Matt. 10:28; 25:41, 46). Man is subject to physical death by God's decree (Heb. 9:27); when death comes, the body will return to the dust, "but the spirit to the God that gave it" (Eccl. 12:7). While the "outward man" is perishing, the "inward man" can be "renewed day by day" (2 Cor. 4:16-18).

The spirit of man in this present life dies in the sense of being separated from God by sin (Isa. 59:2). The Ephesian Christians were once dead in trespasses and sins, but they had been made alive in Christ (Eph. 2:1). While they were "dead" in sins, they were still living, active human beings; they were dead in that they were separated from God by sin — "alienated from the life of God" (Eph. 4:18). Paul described the widow who lives in pleasure as being "dead while she liveth" (1 Tim. 5:6). She was alive physically, dead spiritually. Passages can be multiplied to establish this basic truth.

We need to observe, however, that this spiritual death is not necessarily one of eternal duration. It will be, if the person who is dead in sin is not made alive in Christ. God has provided a way for the spiritually dead to be made alive. Those who are dead *in* sin can be made dead *to* sin through Christ who died *for* sin. In Rom. 6:1-7, Paul explained how and when the "dead" are made "alive."

1. The Roman Christians were dead to sin.
2. They had died to sin when they had been baptized into Christ.
3. When they were baptized into Christ, they were baptized into His death.
4. When they were baptized into the death of Christ, they were baptized into their own death to sin (v. 4).
5. They had been raised, in the likeness of Jesus' resurrection, to newness of life.
6. The old man of sin had been crucified — put to death.
7. They were now dead to and freed from sin.
8. The "dead in sin" had become "dead to sin," and had been made "alive unto God."

We must now understand that this state of being "alive unto God," is not an eternal one, even as being "dead in sin" is not a permanent state. Both states are conditional.

The Alien Sinner

1. If he chooses to remain dead in sin, he is at liberty to do so.

2. If he chooses to be made alive he may; he can then become the servant of righteousness (Eph. 2:1; Rom. 6:17).

3. This change "from death unto life" is effected through obedience to Christ (Jn. 3:5; Matt. 7:21; Heb. 5:8-9; Rom. 6:17).

The Christian

1. If he chooses to remain in that saved relationship with God, he may do so.

2. If he sins (and he will), he has an advocate with God (1 Jn. 2:2).

3. God has a law of pardon for him (Acts 8:22; 1 Jn. 1:7-9).

4. If he decides to continue in sin after baptism, refusing to repent, confess, and ask forgiveness, he becomes dead in sin again.

5. The brother who errs from the truth in any way is a sinner and needs to be converted (Jas. 5:19-20).

The Child of God Has Eternal Life in Promise (1 John 2:25)

A. That promise is contained in God's record (1 John 5:10).

B. Eternal life is promised *in Christ* (1 John 5:11).

C. Jesus has promised eternal life to all who will hear His voice and follow Him (John 10:27-28). It is conditional.

D. That promise will not be fulfilled in this life, but "in the world to come" (Mark 10:30).

The Child of God Has Eternal Life in Hope

A. Paul lived in the hope of eternal life, and that hope was based upon the promise of God (Titus 1:2).

B. The hope of eternal life was made possible by the resurrection of Christ (1 Pet. 1:3-9).

1. There is a salvation which will not be given until the last day (v. 5).

2. It is reserved in *heaven* (v. 4).

3. That reservation is made only for those who are kept by the power of God through faith (v. 5).

4. This salvation is the *end of faith* (v. 9). It is both the aim and the result of faith in Christ.

Salvation Exists in Three Phases

A. Salvation from the past sins of the alien as a result of his obedience to the gospel.

B. A present saved relationship with the Father for the faithful child of God.

C. Eternal salvation (everlasting life) which will be granted to the faithful at the day of judgment.

Concluding Observations

A. If the Child of God has eternal life now, what is left for him to strive for? What reward awaits him in judgment?

B. If eternal life is a present possession, what is it that is "reserved in heaven"?

C. If salvation from past sins for the alien sinner as a result of his primary obedience is everlasting, what is that salvation which will not be granted until the last day?

Questions

In The Light of This Lesson. Explain the Following Passages

A. 1 Timothy 4:1 _____

B. 2 Timothy 2:18 _____

C. 2 Peter 2:19-22 _____

D. Matt. 13:41-42 _____

E. Acts 8:18-23 _____

F. 1 Cor. 15:2 _____

G. Gal. 5:4_____

H. Rom. 8:24-25 _____

I. 2 Peter 1:5-11 _____

Concluding Note

The passages cited in this lesson, it seems to me, are quite sufficient to establish the fact that the Christian can fall from grace and forfeit his right to eternal life. They teach plainly that eternal life is the reward reserved in heaven for the faithful.

Lesson V: The Evolution Of God's Plan

Text

"God, who at sundry times and in divers manners spake in time past unto the fathers by the prophets, hath in these last days spoken unto us by his Son, whom he hath appointed heir of all things, by whom also he made the worlds" (Heb. 1:1-2).

Commentary

In the text above, the apostle stated the basic fact of Divine revelation: "God hath Spoken." He has revealed Himself and His will for men in every dispensation of time. During the period of Old Testament history, God "spake unto the fathers by the prophets;" but that revelation was fragmentary. It was given in many different parts and at various times. Divine revelation came to man as God saw the need for it and as, at the time, He deemed necessary.

As indicated in the introduction to this lesson series, the Divine plan did not come into existence accidentally. It originated as a concept in the mind of God before the worlds were created, and it remained a mystery hidden in His mind until the Holy Spirit revealed and confirmed it in the New Testament (Eph. 3:1-11; 1 Cor. 2:6-14; Rom. 16:25-26). It was with reference to this complete revelation in the New Testament that the Hebrew writer said that God "hath in these last days spoken unto us by his Son" (1:2).

Much of what God spoke "unto the fathers by the prophets" was with reference to and in anticipation of the coming of the Son, His approved life, His death, burial and resurrection, His ascension to the Father's right hand on David's throne, and His present rule in His kingdom, the church, all of which are involved and included in the eternal purpose of God.

In the Old Testament, God promised, prophesied, and set forth in type and in shadow, the "better things" which were to come which things have now been fully revealed in the New Testament. It follows then, that one cannot intelligently study one Testament independently of the other. All things related to the eternal purpose of God in Christ, and about which God "spake unto the fathers by the prophets," can be understood only as they are explained and applied in the New Testament Scriptures.

Peter declared that he (along with James and John) was an eye and ear witness of the transfiguration of Jesus. He said that they were "eyewitnesses of his majesty," and that they heard "the voice from heaven," when the Father acknowledged Jesus as his Son. He further stated that the record which the apostles have given of "the power and coming of our Lord Jesus Christ" is not a fable—not intended to deceive. He affirmed that the testimony of the apostles has made the Old Testament prophecies "more sure."

The important principle announced in this declaration made by Peter is this: Old Testament prophecy was not the product of human wisdom, it did not come to us "by the will of man." It was and is Divine revelation; "holy men of God spake as they were moved by the Holy Ghost." Since Old Testament prophecy was given by inspiration, it must be interpreted (and has been) by inspiration. It is in this sense that "we have also a more sure word of prophecy" (2 Pet. 1:16-21).

No man can ever know the true meaning of the promises, prophecies, and types of the Old Testament except as they are fully explained and applied by Jesus and the inspired writers of the New Testament. There are many Biblical examples of this principle. Some of them are found in the paragraph that follows:

1. Jesus taught Nicodemus that the Brazen Serpent of Num. 21 was typical of His crucifixion (John 3:14-16).

2. Jonah's three days and nights in the whale's belly was a "sign" of Jesus' burial and resurrection (Matt. 12:40).

3. The law of Moses was a shadow of "good things to come" (Heb. 10:1).

4. The Jewish tabernacle was a type of the "true tabernacle which the Lord pitched and not man" (Heb. 8:1-5; Heb. 9:1-11).

5. The "seed of the woman" and the prophecy of Isa. 7:14 was fulfilled and explained by inspiration (Matt. 1:18-25).

6. The "seed" promise to Abraham (Gen. 12) is explained (Gal. 3:16).

7. Joel's prophecy of the baptism of the Holy Spirit (Joel 2:28-32) and Jesus' promise to the apostles (Acts 1:5, 8) is explained by Peter in Acts 2:14-21.

8. Daniel's prophecy of the ascension and enthronement of the Son (Dan.

7:13-14) and David's prophecy of the resurrection of Jesus (Psa. 16:8-11) were fulfilled in Acts 1:9-11 and explained by Peter on Pentecost (Acts 2:25-36).

Many other passages could be given, but these will suffice to show that the true meaning of all of the "shadows" of the Old Testament is found in the "substance" of the New Testament.

God's purpose in Christ by which men are called unto salvation (2 Tim. 1:9; 2 Thess. 2:13-14) has now been accomplished through the preaching of the gospel revealed in the New Testament. Paul said that such preaching was "according to the revelation of the mystery, which was kept secret since the world began, but now is made manifest, and by the *scriptures of the prophets,* according to the commandment of the everlasting God, made known to all nations for the obedience of faith" (Rom. 16:25-26).

God's purpose as thus promised and typified in the Old Testament and revealed in the New, was developed in at least four distinct phases or stages.

I. Promise:

A. The seed of the woman promised in the Garden (Gen. 3:15).

B. The "seed" promise made to Abraham (Gen. 12:3).

C. Thus the gospel was preached to him in promise (Gal. 3:8).

D. That promise was fulfilled in Christ (Gal. 3:16).

E. Christians are "Abraham's seed" and heirs of it (Gal. 3:26-29).

II. Prophecy (1 Pet. 1:8-12):

A. The prophets preached salvation in Christ as they were guided by the Holy Spirit (2 Pet. 1:21).

B. They did not fully understand the things about which they wrote (vs. 10-11). This is an evidence of inspiration.

C. They had no facts at their disposal upon which to base their prophecies; they did not come from their own knowledge, wisdom, or experience.

D. All that was revealed to the prophets concerning the things about which they prophesied, was the fact that their writings were not for benefit of themselves, but for the people of the gospel age, in which age they have been fulfilled, and at which time "all spiritual blessings in Christ" can be enjoyed in "heavenly places" (Eph. 1:1-3).

E. Even the angels desired to understand those prophecies.

III. Preparation:

A. The Ministry of John the Baptist:

1. He was the last Old Testament Prophet before the advent of Christ, the Prophet "like unto Moses" (Deut. 18; Acts 3).

2. He came to bear witness of Christ (Jn. 1:6-7).

3. "Prepare ye the way of the Lord" (Matt. 3:1-5).

4. He preached the baptism of repentance for the remission of sins (Mk. 1:4). His mission was to the Jews who had sinned against the law of Moses and who needed to repent.

5. John did not establish the church; he prepared the material for it. He was the friend of the bridegroom; he had no bride, no church (Jn. 3:28-30).

6. John died before Jesus built His Church. John was never a member of it (Matt. 14:1-12; Matt. 16:18).

7. He that is least in the kingdom of Jesus is greater than John for the above reason (Matt. 11:11).

B. The Personal Ministry of Jesus:

1. His Message: "The time is fulfilled, and the kingdom of God is at hand; Repent ye, and believe the gospel" (Mk. 1:15).

a. The time: the time set by the prophets.

b. The Kingdom: the church of the Lord.

c. At hand: in the near future.

d. Repent ye: the Jews had sinned against the law of Moses.

e. Believe: on Him as the Son of God and accept the gospel of the coming kingdom.

2. His Work:

a. To fulfill all that was written of Him (Matt. 5:17-18).

b. The choosing and training of the twelve.

c. The promise of the Holy Spirit to the apostles (Acts 1:8).

d. He finished His earthly work (John 17:4).

e. His first advent was finished in His death, resurrection and ascension.

IV. Perfection:

A. Pentecost: The Beginning:

1. The apostles were baptized in the Holy Spirit (Acts 2:1-4).

2. The preaching of Christ as Son and Saviour (Acts 2:22-36).

a. His approved life.

b. His death and resurrection.

c. His ascension to the Father.

d. His coronation as king—made both Lord and Christ.

3. Terms of pardon made known to believers (Acts 2:37-39).

4. Three thousand were baptized and added to the Lord on that occasion (Acts 2:41-47).

5. For the first time in history the church was spoken of as being in existence on earth.

6. The Old Testament promises and prophecies respecting the establishment of the church were brought to pass.

B. Subsequent Revelation:

1. The remainder of the Acts of the Apostles.

2. The Epistles written to the church and to individuals.

3. The Revelation.

Questions

1. Why was it that Jesus could not be preached as the Son of God until after His resurrection? _____

_____

2. The apostles could not preach remission of sins in the name of Christ until Pentecost. Give two reasons why.

a. _____

_____

b. _____

_____

3. What was Jesus' first official act as "Lord and Christ"?

_____

4. Why did John the Baptist preach repentance? _____

_____

5. Both John and Jesus preached that the kingdom of God was at hand.

      a. What was the kingdom they referred to? _____

      b. Explain the expression "at hand." _____

6. If John baptized for the remission of sins, why were the twelve disciples at Ephesus required to be baptized in the name of Christ? _____

7. What was the purpose of the baptism of Acts 2:38? ____

8. How would you prove your answer? _____

9. Acts 2:47 teaches that the saved are added to the church, and this means that: _____of the saved were added, _____of the unsaved were added, and _____of the saved were left out of it.

10. Does the church save? _____. Explain:_____

CHAPTER II

Lesson I: Jesus Christ:
Son Of God And Saviour Of The World

Text

"And we have seen and do testify that the Father sent the Son to be the Saviour of the world" (1 Jn. 4:14).

Commentary

Three great truths are stated and implied in the text above:

1. Jesus of Nazareth is the Son of God.
2. The Father sent Him into the world in human form.
3. He came to save men from their sins.

We have observed from the original text of these lessons that God's eternal purpose was in Christ. The scheme of redemption was centered in and waited upon the death and resurrection of Jesus. This fact is clearly set forth in Eph. 1:9-10: "Having made known unto us the mystery of his will, according to his good pleasure which he hath purposed in himself: That in the dispensation of the fulness of times, he might gather together in one all things in Christ, both which are in heaven, and which are in earth; even in him."

All things which are included and involved in the eternal purpose of God were brought to pass in the death and resurrection of Jesus Christ and the subsequent establishment of His church on earth. This divine plan has been recorded and preserved in the New Testament. Paul declares that we can read and understand his "knowledge in the mystery of Christ" (Eph. 3:4). Christians have been saved and called, "not according to our own works, but according to his *purposes* and *grace*, which was given us in *Christ Jesus* before the world began" (2 Tim. 1:9). Salvation is in Christ. God sent His Son to be the Saviour of men.

Facts Related To The Text

A. God promised that the seed of the woman would destroy the power of Satan and sin in the hearts and lives of men (Gen. 3:15).

B. God promised Abraham that He would bless all nations of the world in his seed (Gen. 12:3).

C. Paul identified the promised seed of Abraham as Christ (Gal. 3:16).

D. Christians are of the seed of Abraham by faith (Gal. 3:26-29).

E. Isaiah prophesied that a virgin would bear a son. Thus, the Son would be of the seed of the woman only (Isa. 7:13-14).

F. God's "seed promise" to Abraham and Isaiah's prophecy were fulfilled in the birth of Jesus. His name was called Jesus because He would "*save* his people from their sins" (Matt. 1:18-25).

G. The angels announced His birth as the birth of a *Saviour* (Lk. 2:11).

H. Jesus said that His mission in the world was to seek and to *save* the lost (Lk. 19:10).

I. John summed up all of these facts when he said, "We have seen and do testify that the Father sent the Son to be the Saviour of the world" (1 John 4:14).

J. Finally Paul tells us whom Christ saves. He is the saviour of the body, the church (Eph. 5:23; Col. 1:18). It is essential to note here that the church does not save. Christ is the *Saviour;* the church is the *saved.*

K. Again Paul wrote, "But when the fulness of the time was come, God sent forth his Son, made of a woman, made under the law, to redeem them that were under the law, that we might receive the adoption of sons" (Gal. 4:4-5). Jesus is the Saviour of all men in every age. The Son of God became the son of man, that the sons of men might become the children of God.

Questions

1. Explain the expression "the fulness of times" as used in Eph. 1:9-10 and Gal. 4:4. _____

_____

_____

2. What is the significance of the statement which is made in Matt. 1:24-25? _____

_____

_____

3. How is it possible for Christians to be of the seed of Abraham? _____

4. If Jesus destroyed the power of Satan in His death and resurrection, why do so many people yet live and serve him? __

5. According to Eph. 5:23, who will be saved? _____

6. Does the church save? _____.

7. Explain your answer to question 6: _____

8. In what sense is Jesus the savior of the *world*? _____

Lesson II: The Perfect Saviour

Text

"Though he were a son, yet, learned he obedience by the things which he suffered; And being made perfect, he became the author of eternal salvation unto all them that obey him" (Heb. 5:8-9).

Commentary

If God's perfect plan was to accomplish the end for which it was designed, it would necessarily require a complete and perfect Saviour; that perfection is seen in the person and life of Jesus of Nazareth. From the Bible point of view, one cannot separate the perfect plan from the perfect man. To preach Christ is to preach the plan of salvation offered by Him. To accept the one is to accept the other; to reject the one is to deny the other. Faith in Christ requires faith in the gospel; submission to Christ demands obedience to the gospel. He saves all who will obey Him.

No honest student of the New Testament can fail to see the perfection attributed to and associated with the life of Jesus. On the day of Pentecost, Peter began his sermon at this point: "Ye men of Israel, hear these words; Jesus of Nazareth, a man approved of God among you by miracles and wonders and signs, which God did by him, in the midst of you, as ye yourselves know." He was approved of God, and Peter said this was recognized by the people among whom He lived and to whom He proved His claims by miraculous power (Acts 2:22).

Every trait of His wonderful character, every incident in His sinless life, the complete fulfillment of the promises and prophecies of the Old Testament in His miracles and in His death and resurrection, demonstrate the perfection which the Divine Mind required.

In this lesson we shall examine that perfection as it is related to the following: (A) His relationship with the Father, (B) His sinless earthly life, and (C) His sacrificial death.

Lesson Outline

I. The Perfect Image Of The Father:

A. In the beginning (John 1:1-3, 14; Phil. 2:5-6).

(1) He was the Word (the essence of God).

32

(2) He was with God, and He was God.

(3) He was on an equality with God.

(4) All things were made by Him and for Him.

(5) The Word was made flesh and lived among men.

B. Only the Son could reveal the Father (Matt. 11:27).

C. To see the Son was to see the Father (John 14:8).

D. He possessed every characteristic of God.

II. His Sinless Life:

A. He was never convicted of sin (John 8:46).

B. Though tempted, He did not sin (Heb. 4:15).

C. The lamb was without blemish or spot (1 Pet. 1:19).

D. Because He knew no sin and no guile, He left the perfect example of life (1 Pet. 2:21-22).

E. In the passage above (1 Pet. 1:19-20), Peter declared that Christ, the lamb of God, was foreordained before the foundation of the world; therefore, He was included in God's eternal purpose.

III. His Perfect Sacrifice:

A. Introductory note: When man sinned in the Garden of Eden, he violated the law of heaven. Since the penalty had to be equal to the crime, God imposed the sentence of death upon all men who transgressed His law (Gen. 2:17; Ezek. 18:20). However, the mercy of God intervened in the offering of a heavenly sacrifice. Nothing else could pay the penalty. Vicarious sacrifice, the substitution of the innocent for the guilty, was the only thing which could satisfy the justice of God in the pardon of sin. Since Jesus alone could qualify as the heavenly, sinless sacrifice, God could be just in condemning the sinner and, at the same time, be the justifier of all who believe on Jesus (Rom. 3:26). When God offered up His Son, justice and mercy came to terms at the cross. God so loved the world.

B. Animal sacrifice could not remove sin (Heb. 10:4).

C. Jesus died for transgressions committed under the Old Testament (Heb. 9:15).

D. The New Testament did not become effective until after His death (Heb. 9:16-17).

E. He took away the *first* covenant in order that the *second* might be established (Heb. 10:9-10).

F. His sacrifice was complete and sufficient (Heb. 10:11-14).

G. He died *once*—it was the final sacrifice (Heb. 9:27-28).

H. "There remaineth no more sacrifice. . ." (Heb. 10:26).

Questions

1. Why was the humanity of Jesus essential to His mission as the saviour of the world?

(a) _____ (d) _____
(b) _____ (e) _____
(c) _____

2. In what way was Jesus tempted? _____
_____

3. Name two ways in which Jesus fulfilled the Old Testament law of Moses. (1)_____
(2) _____

4. According to Heb. 10:9-10, what was accomplished by the death of Christ? _____
_____

5. Why could the New Testament plan of salvation *not* become effective until after the death of Christ?_____
_____

6. Explain the meaning of the statement in Heb. 10:26—"There remaineth no more sacrifice for sin." _____
_____

7. Read Heb. 8:11-13 and answer the following questions:
(a) Name two ways in which the New Covenant differs from the Old. _____
_____
_____

(b) What made the first covenant old? _____
_____

Lesson III: The Saviour And The Resurrection

Text

"Now if Christ be preached that he rose from the dead, how say some among you that there is no resurrection of the dead?" (1 Cor. 15:12).

Commentary

There were evidently some among the Corinthian brethren who were questioning the resurrection of the dead. The above text so implies. And so the apostle proceeds to show them that Christ had indeed been raised from the dead and calls to their attention that he had proclaimed the fact of His resurrection as an essential fact of the gospel which he had preached unto them. He further declared that the resurrection of Jesus is the guarantee of ours—a universal resurrection from death.

The resurrection of Jesus was the greatest event in the recorded history of man. It is the very cornerstone of the gospel and the essential truth upon which New Testament Christianity rests. The integrity of the Old Testament prophets, the promises of Jesus Himself, and the truth of the gospel record hinge upon the historical fact of the resurrection of Jesus Christ. The gospel of Christ is a farce and a fraud, "if Christ be not risen" (1 Cor. 15:12-19).

The resurrection of Jesus was the final link in the chain of miraculous events by which He proved His claim to be the Son of God. David foretold His victory over death (Psa. 16:8-11); Peter quoted this prophecy in his sermon at Pentecost to prove that David was speaking, not of himself, but of the resurrection of Christ (Acts 2:25-31). Jesus had told the disciples of His coming death and had promised them that He would rise again on the third day (Matt. 12:40; Mk. 8:31; Jn. 2:19-21). If Jesus did not come forth from the grave, the Scriptures can be broken and He failed to keep His promise. If so, He dealt a death blow to the hope which He had planted in the hearts of His followers.

After His resurrection, Jesus said, "All things must be fulfilled, which are written in the law of Moses, and in the prophets, and in the psalms concerning me." Among those things which had been written concerning Him was the fact that "it behooved Christ to suffer, and to rise from the dead the third day: and that repentance and remission of sins should be preached in his name . . ." (Lk. 24:44-47). Thus, the preaching of the gospel waited on the resurrection of Christ, even as Isaiah had said (Isa. 2:1-5). In his sermon at Antioch of Pisidia, Paul taught that the dead body of Jesus was not removed from the cross until "they had fulfilled all that had been written of Him." Up to that time, "all things" had been accomplished "according to the Scriptures." From that hour the hope of mankind waited on His resurrection; but that hope was not in vain: "But God raised him from the dead: And he was seen many days of them which came up with him from Galilee to Jerusalem, who are his witnesses unto the people" (Acts 13:29-31). The prophets foretold His resurrection, witnesses testified that they had seen Him alive after His death, and Paul preached their testimony.

Jesus was declared to be the Son of God by His resurrection from the dead (Rom. 1:4). Men had been crucified before and people had been raised from the dead prior to the time that Joseph's tomb was found to be empty; but those individuals lived to keep the appointment with physical death again. Jesus was raised to die no more—"death hath no more dominion over him." Forty days later He went back to the Father in the clouds of heaven while the apostles viewed the ascension with wonder (Acts 1:9-11).

The death, burial and resurrection of Jesus constitute the basic facts of the gospel of Christ (1 Cor. 15:1-4). One cannot believe the gospel and deny the resurrection of Jesus. His resurrection is no less important to our faith than is His sacrificial death. Leave out the resurrection, and you destroy the gospel as the power of God unto salvation. Without it, faith is vain and baptism is meaningless.

Access to the grace of God, remission of sins by the shed blood of Jesus, the blessed hope of life after death in an eternal abode with God, etc. depend upon the historical fact of the resurrection of God's Son. The grandest thought that can fill the mind of the Christian and the greatest assurance that can be given to him, is the confidence that he serves a risen Lord who "ever liveth to make intercession for them" (Heb. 7:25).

Since so many people in our day approach the study of the resurrection with a skeptical attitude and with little faith in the Bible account of it, perhaps the best way to convince the gainsayer, is to appeal to his reason by asking him certain questions which are unanswerable, if the Bible record of the resurrection is not true.

1. What became of the body? Why the empty tomb? What of the napkin that lay by itself?

2. Who rolled the stone from the mouth of the tomb?

3. How could the soldiers who guarded the tomb testify that His disciples stole the body while they slept? If they were asleep, how could they know what happened to it?

4. Why did the enemies of Jesus not expose the error of those who preached the resurrection, if it did not occur?

5. Why did so many of the Jews who hated and rejected the Saviour, like Saul of Tarsus, turn from the Jewish religion to preach the faith they once sought to destroy?

6. Would the apostles of our Lord and countless other Christians have given their lives for the cause of one who lied to them?

7. Why has the fact of the resurrection stood unshaken for two thousand years, and influenced with incomparable impact the hearts and lives of men and the history of nations?

Questions

A. The Witnesses:

1. Jesus appeared first to _____(Mk. 16:9).

2. Luke lists the following people who witnessed the empty tomb: _____, _____, _____and _____(Lk. 24:1-10).

3. Paul mentions the following people who saw Jesus alive after His resurrection: _____, _____, _____, _____, _____, _____, _____, (1 Cor. 15:5-9).

B. Some Results if there is No Resurrection (1 Cor. 15:12-19).

1._____

2._____

3._____

4._____

5._____

6._____

7._____

C. Supply The Information Called For (1 Cor. 15):

1. In this same chapter Paul teaches a universal resurrection based upon _____.

2. Jesus will _____ until the last enemy, _____, is destroyed by the _____.

3. When Paul said that all things had been put in subjection to Jesus, he gave one exception. Who was it?_____

4. Explain v. 29: _____

_____

5. Explain v. 49: _____

_____

6. The "mystery" which Paul showed the Corinthians was that both the living and the dead will _____ at the time of the universal resurrection.

7. This will be necessary because flesh and blood _____

_____.

8. Christians will be given a _____ body.

9. Do we know just what the new body will be? _____ (Give the passage.)_____

CHAPTER III
Lesson I: Salvation In Christ
Text
"Therefore I endure all things for the elect's sake, that they may also obtain the salvation which is in Christ Jesus with eternal glory" (2 Tim. 2:10).

Commentary
The text states in no uncertain terms that salvation is in Jesus Christ. The apostle further states that he endured all of the persecution and oppression imposed upon him as the apostle to the Gentiles that others might enjoy the same salvation which he enjoyed in Christ—all of the blessings and privileges which the Christian receives in this present life and the promise and hope of eternal life in the world to come.

God has promised Abraham that He would bless all nations in his seed; that seed is Christ (Gal. 3:16). Therefore, God's promise is fulfilled and His blessings enjoyed in Christ. Again, in our original text (Eph. 3:11), God's eternal purpose is said to be in Christ. Further, the apostle affirmed that God would, according to His purpose, "gather together in one, all things in Christ." The "all things" of this passage comprehends all spiritual provisions promised through the lineage of Abraham. Everything included and involved in the gospel plan was completed and brought to pass in Christ. Jehovah makes no provision for the souls of men outside of Christ. All spiritual blessings are in Him (Eph. 1:3).

Study the Charts Below:
The Blessings in Christ

Redemption	Eph. 1:7
Reconciliation	2 Cor. 5:18-20
New Creatures	2 Cor. 5:17
All Spiritual Blessings	Eph. 1:3
The Promises of God	2 Cor. 1:20
The Hope of Eternal Life	1 Cor. 15:19

All are made one Children of God Seed of Abraham Heirs of Promise	Gal. 3:26-29

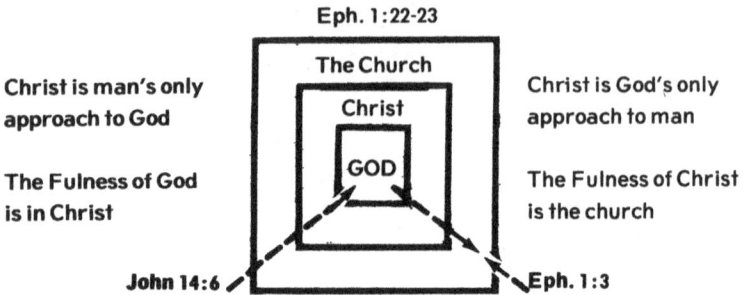

Eph. 1:22-23

```
                    ┌─────────────────┐
                    │  The Church     │
 Christ is man's only │  ┌──────────┐ │    Christ is God's only
 approach to God    │  │  Christ   │ │    approach to man
                    │  │ ┌──────┐  │ │
 The Fulness of God │  │ │ GOD  │  │ │    The Fulness of Christ
 is in Christ       │  │ └──────┘  │ │    is the church
                    │  └──────────┘ │
  John 14:6         └─────────────────┘    Eph. 1:3
```

Questions

1. How may both Jew and Gentile become the children of God? _____

_____

2. How many are the children of God by faith? _____

_____

3. How does one put on Christ? _____

_____

4. Why is it true that one can believe in the Divinity of Christ, repent of every sin, confess the name of Christ, and still not be *in* Christ? _____

_____

5. Is it possible for one to be in Christ and not be in the church? _____. Explain: _____

_____

6. Explain why baptism is essential in order for one to reach the blood of Christ (John 19:33-34; Rom. 6:3-4). _____

_____

_____

7. What does *reconciliation* mean? _____

8. How was it made possible? _____

9. Where does it take place? _____

_____(Col. 1:20; Eph. 2:16).

Concluding note on Christ and the Church:

When one is baptized into Christ, he is added to the church. To be in

Christ is to be in the church; but the church does not save. Jesus is the *savior;* the church is the saved. The church is composed of all who have been saved from past sins *by* Christ.

Lesson II: The Great Salvation
Text
"Therefore,we ought to give the more earnest heed to the things which we have heard, lest at any time we should let them slip. For if the word spoken by angels was stedfast, and every transgression and disobedience received a just recompense of reward; how shall we escape, if we neglect so great salvation; which at the first began to be spoken by the Lord, and was confirmed unto us by them that heard him" (Heb. 2:1-3).

Commentary

Perhaps there is no one word which better describes the salvation which is in Christ than the word *great.* Salvation means deliverance, and there are many Old Testament examples of God's deliverance of His people in ages past. These examples have been recorded for our learning (Rom. 15:4); they serve as types and shadows of the great salvation in Christ. However, as one studies these examples in the Old Testament, one will observe that none of them is referred to as a *great* salvation.

By way of contrast, the apostle to the Hebrews sets forth the principle by which God has dealt with men in every age. In the Old Testament Age, every violation of God's law carried with it a just penalty and every case of obedience to that law brought forth a blessing upon the individual who thus obeyed. It is in this context that the writer warns us not to neglect the salvation offered by the Lord. If the word of God spoken by angels stood firmly, the greater message spoken by the Son must also stand. None who neglect the word of salvation spoken by him, can escape from the just penalty of his transgressions.

Some Reasons Why It Is A Great Salvation

I. Jesus Christ is the author of it:

    A. It was first spoken by Him (Text).

    B. He is greater than the Old Testament prophets (Matt. 17:1-11).

    C. He is greater than Moses (Heb. 3:1-6).

    D. He is God's spokesman for this age (Heb. 2:1-2).

II. Because of What is Involved:

A. It is *not* just temporal and temporary.

B. It involves the immortal spirit of man (Matt. 16:26).

C. It is release from the guilt of sin (Eph. 1:7).

D. It is an eternal salvation (Heb. 5:8-9).

E. There is no escape, if we neglect it (Text).

III. Because of the Cost:

A. It cost God His Son (John 3:14-16).

B. It cost the Son His life (John 15:13).

C. We were purchased with His blood (Acts 20:28).

D. It has cost the sacrifices of faithful members to maintain and preserve the New Testament church.

E. It will cost Christians today:

(1) Self-denial (Matt. 16:24).

(2) Separation from the world (2 Cor. 6:14-18).

(3) It demands the proper use of our talents, wealth, time and opportunities.

IV. The Threat of Great Punishment:

A. The penalty is great (Heb. 10:28-29).

B. Eternal separation from God (2 Thess. 1:7-9).

C. Everlasting fire (Matt. 25:41).

D. Eternal death—the lake of fire (Rev. 20:12-15).

V. Because of Its Promises:

A. They are exceeding great and precious (2 Pet. 1:3-4).

B. Through them we can partake of God's nature (2 Pet. 1:3-4).

C. Four great promises for the obedient:

(1) Remission of our sins (Acts 2:38-39).

(2) Gift of the Holy Spirit (Acts 2:38-39).

(3) All spiritual blessing now (Eph. 1:3).

(4) Eternal life in heaven (1 John 2:25).

Questions

1. What was the purpose of the miracles mentioned in Heb. 2:1-4?_____

_____

2. Give two reasons why such miracles are not now possible: _____

_____

3. The text states that the great salvation was first spoken by the Lord. At what point in time did this take place?_____

_____

4. Give some Old Testament examples where "transgression and disobedience received a just recompense of reward." _____

_____

_____

5. Give some Old Testament examples of God's deliverance of His people: _____

_____

6. In Heb. 11:7 we are told that Noah and his house were saved by faith while Gen. 6:8 indicates that it was a matter of grace. Explain: _____

_____

_____

Lesson III: The Common Salvation

Text

"Beloved, when I gave all diligence to write unto you of the common salvation, it was needful for me to write unto you, and exhort you that ye should earnestly contend for the faith which was once delivered to the saints" (Jude 3).

Commentary

The context of Jude 3 indicates that certain false teachers had "crept in unawares," unobserved and unannounced. The false teacher does not identify himself as such; he comes as a "wolf in sheep's clothing." Once he gets into the church and gains the confidence of the brethren, many are led away from the faith as a result of his work. Jude's admonition of the saints was a charge for them to stand with fervor and faith against this invasion of error. It was a charge that was needful in the first century, and has continued to be a constant need of the church, individually and collectively, in every generation.

It is significant, I think, that in exhorting Christians to contend for the faith, he was writing to them concerning the *common salvation.* The common salvation is based upon and grows out of a common faith—a common doctrine, the gospel of Christ. It is a common salvation because it is that salvation which is offered to all men upon the same terms for all time to come.

God is no respector of persons; He has provided one plan for all men. That plan has been revealed in the New Testament—a common salvation revealed in the common faith. God does not save one man by one plan and another individual by some other means. No man has a plan or a church of his choice. God has provided only one arrangement, and that for all men (Eph. 4:1-6). All who accept that plan can and will be one in Christ. All who reject the plan reject God and His son. The only choice men have in the matter is to receive or reject the plan.

Religious division as it exists today is a repudiation of the prayer of Christ (John 17:20-21). It makes the death of Christ of no effect (Eph. 2:14-16). Paul argued that, if men could be saved by the law, then Jesus died in vain (Gal. 2:21). The same apostle said, "Now I beseech you, brethren, by the name of our Lord Jesus Christ, that ye all speak the same thing, and that there be no divisions among you; but that ye be perfectly joined together in the same mind, and in the same judgment" (1 Cor. 1:10). Religious division, therefore, stands in open violation to a command of an inspired apostle of Jesus Christ.

There is no verse in the New Testament which justifies religious division. Denominationalism rests upon a human foundation. It exists without Divine sanction, and it is no part of the "common salvation" in Christ.

Some Elements of the Common Salvation

A. It meets the common need of all men (Rom. 3:23).

B. It required a common sacrifice (Heb. 2:9).

C. It demands a common authority (1 Cor. 1:10).

D. It is obtained in a common body (Eph. 5:23).

E. It has a common objective (1 Pet. 1:8-10).

The Teaching of Jesus

A. He promised to build one church (Matt. 16:18).

B. He promised one fold and one shepherd (John 10:16).

C. He Prayed that all believers might be one (John 17:20-21).

D. He died that both Jew and Gentile might be at peace with God in one body (Eph. 2:14-16).

E. The plan of salvation announced at Pentecost promised salvation on common terms for all men and for all time (Acts 2:38-39).

The Common Plan Explained (Eph. 4:1-6)

The seven ones of this text comprehend every provision which the grace of God has made for human redemption. They constitute the Christian's religious platform. Upon them he must stand, and in them his faith and hope must be planted. It is important to observe also, that men are prone to accept a part of the whole while disregarding the remainder. This simply cannot be done; it is all or none. All of them must stand or fall together. To leave out any one of the seven is to destroy the

completeness of the Divine Plan. Study the text and supply
the information called for in the outline below:

    A. One God suggests a unity of _____ (John 4:24).

    B. One Lord demands but one _____ (Matt. 28:18).

    C. One Spirit has given but one _____ (1 Cor. 2:10).

    D. One faith means one system of _____ (Jude 3).

    E. One body has reference to the _____ (Col. 1:18).

    F. One baptism represents the one means of _____
into the body (1 Cor. 10:13).

    G. The one hope is the hope of _____ (Titus 1:2).

Questions

1. In the passage just studied, what effort is required of all
Christians? _____

2. What attitude is essential, if that effort is to be effective? _____

_____

3. In what sense was Paul a prisoner of Jesus Christ for the
Gentiles? _____

_____

4. In the light of the passage mentioned, what is your answer to the statement that "one church is as good as another"?

_____

5. What is the nature of the unity for which Christ prayed
in the prayer of John 17? _____

_____

6. According to Jesus' prayer, how was the unity of faith
to be realized? _____

_____

7. In Eph. 2:14-16, Paul stated that Jesus made of the Jew
and Gentile "one new man." To what does this expression
refer? _____

_____

8. What was accomplished through the death of Christ
that made this possible? _____

_____

9. Name some causes of continued religious division? _____

_____

_____

10. What is the cure for division in the religious world at large and within the body of Christ? _____

_____

Lesson IV: The Conditional Salvation

Text

"Though he were a son, yet learned he obedience by the things which he suffered: And being made perfect, he became the author of eternal salvation unto all them that obey him" (Heb. 5:8-9).

Commentary

The text affirms that salvation in Christ is conditional. The promise of salvation is conditioned upon man's obedience. The individual who has not obeyed the Lord cannot claim Him as personal savior. Jesus offers salvation to all men (Matt. 11:28-30). He has made adequate provision for all men by His sacrifice (1 John 2:1-2). However, He demands obedience on the part of all men if they are to receive freedom from the guilt and the stain of sin.

Since God is the creator of man, the system which He devised had to be consistent with the nature of man as God made him to be. Having been fashioned in the image of the Creator, man was endowed with certain faculties which had to be exercised in the determination of his destiny. Thus, man was meant to be an active agent in his own salvation. The justice of God, therefore, required that certain conditions be set forth in order for men to employ the power of choice.

Both the nature of God and the nature of man necessitated a conditional plan of redemption.

I. *The Nature of God:*

A. God is omniscient, He knew the nature and needs of man.

B. His love and mercy was universal; His plan had to be extended to all mankind.

C. There is no respect of persons with God; He imposes the same conditions upon all.

D. If the love and mercy of God offers release from the guilt of sin, the justice of God demands punishment for all who reject that offer.

II. *The Nature Of Man:*

A. He has an intellect to understand and believe the Father's revealed will.

B. He is blessed with volition, the power of choice, to reject or accept that revelation.

C. He possesses emotions which enable him to enjoy the blessings of salvation or to suffer remorse of conscience for his transgressions.

III. *The Gospel Is In Harmony With Man's Nature:*

A. The facts of the gospel appeal to the intellect.

B. The commands of the gospel call for the exercise of will.

C. The glorious promises and the terrible threats found in the gospel stir his emotions.

Questions

I. *The Plan For The Alien Sinner:*

A. Requires Understanding:

(1) The sinner must hear in order to_____
_____(Rom. 10:14).

(2) Jesus said one must hear and _____
_____(John 6:45).

(3) The sinner must have knowledge of _____
_____ (John 8:32).

B. Faith is Essential:

(1) Faith in _____(Heb. 11:6).

(2) Faith in _____ (John 8:24).

(3) Faith in _____ (Mark 16:15-16).

C. Repentance is Necessary:

(1) The sinner must repent or he will _____
_____(Luke 13:3).

(2) All men are commanded to _____
_____(Acts 17:30).

(3) God would have all men come to _____
_____(2 Pet. 3:9).

(4) Repentance is defined as a _____
_____(Matt. 21:28-29).

(5) The change of number 4 leads to _____
_____(Jonah 3:10).

(6) Men are led to repentance by:

(a) _____ (Rom. 2:4).

(b) _____ (2 Cor. 7:10).

(c) _____ (Acts 17:30-31).

D. Confession is a Condition:

(1) It is a confession with the _____ (Rom. 10:9).

(2) It is a confession unto _____ (Rom. 10:10).

(3) Made in the presence of _____ (Matt. 10:32).

(4) Confession of the sonship of _____ (Matt. 16:16).

E. The Essentiality of Baptism:

(1) Baptism is for (unto) the _____
_____(Acts 2:38).

(2) In order to have our sins _____ (Acts 22:16).

(3) Baptism puts one into _____ (Rom. 6:3).

(4) Baptism puts one into _____ (1 Cor. 12:13).

(5) In baptism one puts on _____ (Gal. 3:27).

(6) In baptism we receive _____ (Col. 2:12).

(7) The action of baptism is _____ (Rom. 6:4).

(8) In baptism we are raised _____
_____(Rom. 6:4).

(9) In baptism we are made _____
_____(Rom. 6:7).

(Note: In the light of the above evidence to the contrary, how could one possibly conclude that baptism is not essential to salvation from sin?)

II. *God's Plan For The Erring Christian:*

A. The Christian is to walk (live) by _____ (2 Cor. 5:7).

B. He is expected to be faithful in _____(Heb. 10:25).

C. His life is to become _____ (Phil. 1:27).

D. In the use of his time, talents and opportunities, the Christian is to be _____ (Matt. 25:14-21).

E. The Christian has an advocate with _____ and that advocate is_____(1 John 2:1).

F. If and when the Christian sins, he is:

(1) Commanded to _____ (Acts 8:22).

(2) Told to ask in _____ (John 14:13).

(3) To be willing to _____ (Matt. 6:12).

(4) To ask according _____ (1 John 5:14).

(5) The Christian will receive what he asks if, _____
_____(1 John 3:22).

Concluding Note

There are two laws of pardon in the New Testament — one

for the alien sinner, and one for the Christian. Each law must
be applied to the one for whom it was given. Men often apply
God's plan for the Christian to the alien sinner. To do so is to
misrepresent the word of God. The false teacher who tells sin-
ners outside of Christ, to "repent and pray," handles the word
of God "deceitfully." One law cannot replace the other, nor under any circumstances be substituted for it.

CHAPTER IV
Lesson I: The Mystery Revealed
Text

"... If ye have heard of the dispensation of the grace of God which is given me to you-ward: How that by revelation he made known unto me the mystery; (as I wrote afore in few words, whereby, when ye read, ye may understand my knowledge in the mystery of Christ) which in other ages was not made known unto the sons of men, as it is now revealed unto his holy apostles and prophets by the Spirit" (Eph. 3:2-5).

Commentary

The gospel plan was a mystery hidden in the mind of God throughout the ages of the Old Testament. It had been revealed only in promise and prophecy and in the types and shadows of the Old Testament. The prophets who foretold its advent did not understand the true meaning of those things which were to come to pass about which they prophesied (1 Pet. 1:10-12).

However, in the text above, the apostle declared that the mystery has now been revealed by the Spirit. He further stated that his mission as an apostle to the Gentiles was "to make all men see what is the fellowship of the mystery, which from the beginning of the world hath been hid in God, who created all things by Jesus Christ." He would accomplish this by preaching "the unsearchable riches of Christ"—the gospel.

God's perfect plan *for* man demanded a revelation of that plan *to* man. The gospel of Christ is that complete revelation, and it is the power of God to save (Rom. 1:16). Since the plan of God in Christ is conditional, both the justice of God and the nature of man dictated a clear and complete revelation of those conditions. Furthermore, because the gospel is a universal message from God upon which the redemption of the race depended, it was essential that it be made known in simple language which could be read and understood by responsible men in all walks and on all levels of life.

The New Testament is that perfect revelation of the will of God and the duty of man for this dispensation of time. It admits of no error nor does it allow for addition, subtraction or revision of any kind. No other plan or system of religion can be substituted for it. The New Testament is perfect and complete in the following ways: (1) It is the inspired and confirmed word of God. (2) It contains all that Jehovah would have men to know in order to be saved eternally, and it is sufficient to supply every spiritual need of mankind. (3) It is God's final message to humanity.

Facts Set Forth In The Text:

A. The mystery was made known to Paul by revelation.

B. That revelation had come as a result of the dispensation of the grace of God. It is the gospel of grace.

C. It has been written in words which can be understood.

D. We can now know what Paul knew by inspiration.

E. The Jew and Gentile would share equally in its provisions:

(1) The Gentiles would be fellow-heirs with the Jews.

(2) They would be fellow-members of the same body.

(3) They would be fellow-partakers of the same promise.

Questions

(1) In what sense was Paul a prisoner of Jesus Christ for the Gentiles? _____

_____

2. Paul describes himself as "less than the least of all saints." Explain why: _____

_____

3. How is the gospel of Christ related to the grace of God?

_____

4. Explain the connection between the New Testament and the Holy Spirit. _____

_____

5. How does the Holy Spirit speak to men today? _____

_____

6. Who are the prophets referred to in the text? _____

_____

7. Why was their work essential in the first century?_____

_____

8. When did their work cease? _____

_____

Lesson II: Divine Revelation Explained
(A study of 1 Corinthians 2)
Commentary

It is evident from 1 Cor. 15:1-3 and from Acts 18:8 that Paul had preached the gospel in Corinth, and that "many of the Corinthians hearing, believed, and were baptized." This epistle, therefore, was written to individuals who had thus obeyed the gospel. The apostle, referring to the time when he had preached there, indicated that he had made known to them the mystery which we studied about in Lesson I. Note the facts stated in verses 1-9:

A. The source of his preaching was not human wisdom.

B. He proclaimed to them God's testimony of His Son.

C. He knew nothing among them "save Jesus Christ, and Him crucified."

D. The reason: that their faith might not stand in human wisdom, but in the power of God—the gospel.

E. He had preached "the wisdom of God in a mystery."

F. This wisdom was ordained before the world began.

G. It remained a mystery until it was revealed by the Holy Spirit in the New Testament:

(1) Eye had not seen it; it had not been written.

(2) Ear had not heard it; it had not been proclaimed.

(3) Therefore, the hearts of men had not understood the provisions that God had made for mankind in the gospel of His Son.

The Need For Divine Revelation

A. Man cannot know God's will by human wisdom (1 Cor. 1:21).

B. We are able to know the mind of God only as He wills to make it known to us (Rom. 11:33-36; 1 Cor. 2:11).

C. Man is a responsible being with a mind to understand and a will to act.

D. The love and the justice of God demand that He disclose His will in order for man to decide his destiny.

E. Man is inherently religious. He needed the object of his worship revealed to him.

The Process Examined (1 Cor. 2:10-14)

A. *The Source:* God.

1. God has revealed the "things" of verse 9 (verse 10).

2. Otherwise man cannot know "the things of God" (verse 11).

B. *The Agent:* The Holy Spirit.

1. God has revealed them by the Spirit (verse 10).

2. Only the Spirit knew the mind of God (verse 11).

3. Therefore, only the Spirit could reveal it to man.

4. The apostles had received the Spirit of God in order to know "the things of God" (verse 12).

C. *The Means of Communication:* Language.

1. "Which things we speak" (verse 13).

2. Their words chosen by the Spirit (verse 13).

3. These "things of God" have been written (Eph. 3:4).

4. *Note:* Things revealed by the Spirit in words chosen by the Spirit constitute verbal inspiration.

D. *The End Result:* The New Testament.

1. It is the source of spiritual knowledge (verse 14).

2. It enables us to discern good and evil (Heb. 5:12-14).

Questions

1. Define *revelation:* _____

_____

2. Define *inspiration:* _____

_____

3. What passage in this chapter teaches the verbal inspiration of the New Testament? _____

_____

4. Why did Paul determine to know nothing "save Christ and him crucified?" _____

_____

5. In preaching Christ unto them, what facts did he present (1 Cor. 15)?_____

_____

6. What is the significance of the expression "according to the scriptures"? _____

_____

7. Explain 1 Cor. 2:9. _____

_____

8. What was the grace of God given unto Paul which enabled him to lay the foundation at Corinth (1 Cor. 3:10)? ____

_____

9. What foundation did he lay? _____

_____.

10. What did the Corinthian Christians do in order to be built upon that foundation (Acts 18:8)? _____

_____.

Lesson III: The Testimony Of The Apostles

The Apostleship

A. *Apostle:* One who is sent.

    1. John was an apostle of God (John 1:6).

    2. Jesus was an apostle of God (Heb. 3:1).

    3. The twelve were apostles of Christ (Matt. 10:1-5).

B. *The apostles of Christ:*

    1. They were the original earthen vessels (2 Cor. 4:7).

    2. They were witnesses of Christ (Acts 1:8).

    3. They were ambassadors of Christ (2 Cor. 5:20).

    4. They were given the word of God (John 17:8).

    5. They spoke those things which they had seen and heard (Acts 4:19-20).

Examples of Apostolic Testimony

A. *The Testimony of Peter:* (2 Pet. 1:16-21).

    1. Peter and the other apostles have made known the power and coming of Christ.

    2. This revelation was not a fable—not intended to deceive.

    3. Peter, James and John were eye and ear witnesses of the transfiguration of Christ.

    4. They heard the voice of God from heaven as He declared Jesus to be His Son.

    5. Old Testament prophecies concerning Christ have been confirmed by their testimony.

B. *The Testimony of John:* John 20:19-31.

    1. John and the other apostles were witnesses of the bodily presence of Jesus after His resurrection.

    2. It was on this occasion that Thomas confessed Christ.

    3. According to John's record, the faith of Thomas was based on sight.

    4. Our faith must be based upon the testimony of these who were eye and ear witnesses. Christians are "they who have not seen, and yet have believed."

    5. The record of this miracle and others written in John's gospel have been recorded to produce faith in Christ.

C. *The Testimony of Paul* (Gal. 1:11-17; 2:1-7; 1 Cor. 15:1-5):

    1. He had seen Jesus after His resurrection.

    2. He did not receive the gospel from men.

    3. He had not been taught by the other apostles.

    4. It was given to him by revelation.

    5. He went to Jerusalem and preached the gospel by revelation.

    6. He proclaimed the same gospel to the Gentiles that Peter preached to the Jews.

Questions

    1. What was the basic qualification for the apostleship? __
_____

    2. During what period of time did the original twelve meet this qualification? _____
_____(Acts 1:22)

    3. Why was it necessary that an apostle be selected on the occasion of question 2? _____
_____

    4. What was the one exception to the rule stated in your answer to question 2? _____

    5. Why did Jesus appear to Saul on the road to Demascus?
_____(Acts 26:16)

    6. Is it possible for one to be an apostle today? _____
_____

    7. Why?_____

    8. How would you classify the Mormon apostles? _____
_____

Lesson IV: The Sufficiency Of Revelation
Commentary

If the New Testament was to represent the will of God for man and if the salvation of man depended upon it, it had to be sufficient to meet the spiritual needs of all men. To say otherwise is to reflect upon the widsom and the power of God. God is the creator of both the body and the spirit of man. He has made adequate provision for both in His own way. The gospel of Christ is God's means of providing for the spiritual man; it makes the claim of absolute perfection and completeness. One cannot improve upon it even as one cannot improve upon the sinless life of Jesus or upon the perfect sacrifice which He offered on the cross.

Faith in the sufficiency of the New Testament demands a total rejection of all human creeds which have been written to supplement and replace it. These human documents must be rejected for many reasons:

1. They exist without the authority of God.

2. They are no more infallible than the men who wrote them.

3. All of them either add to or take from the doctrine of Christ and, thus, become sinful (2 John 9-10).

4. Changes in theological thought have brought about changes in human creeds. The word of God abides forever (1 Pet. 1:25).

5. Many of these creeds are being amended and revised to accommodate the changing attitudes of the masses on many moral and spiritual issues. In such cases, the voice of the people becomes the voice of God to all who accept them.

6. They encourage and promote religious division which the New Testament condemns.

7. Human creeds are powerless to save the soul.

The Sufficiency of Inspired Scripture

I. *2 Timothy 3:14-17:*

A. Timothy had known the Holy Scriptures from childhood.

B. These Old Testament Scriptures had given him the knowledge of salvation through faith in Christ.

C. The Old Testament forms the initial basis of our faith in Christ. They testify of Him (John 5:39).

D. Inspired Scripture is sufficient for:

1. Doctrine: the source of spiritual knowledge.

2. Reproof: exposure of doctrinal error and sin.

3. Correction: it is the means for correcting our mistakes.

4. Instruction in righteous living.

E. The man of God is (1) made complete and (2) given a pattern for the good works which the Father requires.

II. *2 Peter 1:3-4:*

A. God has given us access to the knowledge of Christ.

B. By that knowledge we can escape the corruption of sin.

C. Through it we can know all things which relate to godly living and the hope of eternal life.

D. By faith in its promises, we can be made partakers of the nature of God.

III. *James 1:18-25*

A. We are begotten spiritually by the engrafted word. It is the seed of the kingdom (Luke 8:11). There is no other source of spiritual life (John 6:63).

B. It is a mirror into which one can look and see oneself as God sees and knows him to be.

C. It is the perfect law of liberty:

1. It is the *law* of Christ.

2. It is a *perfect* (complete) law.

3. It is the law of *liberty.* Men can be made free from sin through knowledge of it and obedience to it.

IV. *The New Testament in Faith and Practice:*

A. It is the ground of our faith (Rom. 10:17).

B. It is the only basis of unity (1 Cor. 1:10).

C. It is the rule for our worship (John 4:24).

D. It is the source of our edification (Acts 20:32).

E. It sets the pattern for righteous conduct (Phil. 1:27).

F. It will be the standard of judgment (John 12:48).

Questions

1. Where and how had Timothy learned the Holy Scriptures? _____

_____

2. What implications does your answer have for us? _____

_____

3. How would you define a good work (2 Tim. 3:16-17)? ____

_____

4. What is our obligation with regard to such work? _____
_____(Titus 3:1, 8; Eph. 2:10)

5. When one looks into the perfect law of Christ, upon what condition is one blessed? _____

_____

Lesson V: The Finality Of Revelation

Text

"Beloved, when I gave all diligence to write unto you of the common salvation, it was needful for me to write unto you, and exhort you that ye should earnestly contend for the faith which was once delivered unto the saints" (Jude 3).

Commentary

We have observed elsewhere in these lessons that revelation was delivered to man as the need for such revelation arose. It is evident from the above text that Jude had written this epistle because there was a definite need for it. The purpose for which the letter was written was discussed in a previous lesson.

We are presently concerned with that part of the text which declares the finality of Divine Revelation. Jude affirmed that the "faith" has been *once* delivered. The "faith" of this text is objective faith. It has to do with the doctrine believed, rather than the process of giving mental assent to a given set of facts. Jude asserted that the "faith" has been finalized and delivered in complete form. The "faith" is simply God's perfect plan revealed and recorded in the New Testament. Thus, Jude claimed the finality of revelation as opposed to the idea of continued revelation as exposed by various religious groups today.

Jesus promised the apostles that the Holy Spirit would come and guide them into *all* truth (John 16:13). Did the Holy Spirit complete His work of revelation or did He fail in His mission? If He accomplished His task, the "faith" which has been delivered contains all truth which God deemed essential to our salvation. No further revelation is needed and none will be given. The New Testament is the Lord's final message to humanity.

The gospel plan for the alien sinner was first announced at Pentecost. Peter preached that remission of sins in the name of Christ would be granted to all succeeding generations of Jews and Gentiles upon the same terms set forth on that occasion.

There would be no changes made. Moreover, in the subsequent chapters of Acts and in the New Testament epistles, we are instructed in all things which are necessary for the Christian to know and do in the living of an acceptable life. The New Testament is the only rule of faith and practice in directing our lives in worship and service to God. We are forbidden to add to or take from it (Rev. 22:18-19). The curse of God rests upon all who would pervert it in any form or fashion (Gal. 1:6-9). It represents God's will for man in complete and final form.

Lesson Outline

I. *The Faith:*

    A. It is the New Testament—the source of authority.

    B. It is inspired, confirmed, complete and final.

II. *Delivered:* by the authorized representatives of Christ.

    A. *The Apostles:*

        1. They were His witnesses (Acts 1:8).

        2. They were His ambassadors (2 Cor. 5:18-20).

        3. They had binding and losing power (Matt. 16:19).

        4. Christ gave them His Word (John 17:8).

    B. There were other inspired writers besides the apostles.

III. *Once Delivered:*

    A. Delivered *one* time for *all* time.

    B. *Once,* the same word as appears in Heb. 9:27-28.

IV. *To the Saints:*

    A. Every Christian is a saint (Phil. 1:1).

    B. A saint is one who has been sanctified (1 Cor. 1:1-2).

    C. God has entrusted His Word to our care and keeping.

    D. We are responsible for its proclamation in word and deed.

V. *Contend For It:*

    A. We are obligated to defend it against all error.

    B. We are to be set for the defense of the gospel (Phil. 1:17).

    C. We must fight the good fight of faith (1 Tim. 6:12).

Questions

1. In the light of this lesson, what would you say of the doctrine of continued revelation? _____

_____

2. Is this a new idea? _____(Rev. 2:2)

3. Give some present-day examples of "continued revelation." _____

_____

4. Give some reasons why men cannot receive revelation from God in addition to the New Testament: _____

_____

_____

5. Name some New Testament writers who were not apostles. _____

_____

6. The word *faith* is used in two ways in the New Testament: Explain. _____

_____

_____

Lesson VI: The Authority Of Revelation

Text

"And when he was come into the temple, the chief priests and the elders of the people came unto him as he was teaching, and said, By what authority doest thou these things? and who gave thee this authority? And Jesus answered and said unto them, I also will ask you one thing, which if ye tell me, I in like wise will tell you by what authority I do these things. The baptism of John, whence was it? from heaven, or of men?" (Matt. 21:23-24).

Commentary

When the priests and elders asked the question recorded in the text above, they asked the question which any person has the right to ask of another with regard to his or her religious faith and practice. The genuine Christian will always welcome any challenge to his faith; he will be grateful for the opportunity to "give an answer to every man that asketh you the reason of the hope that is in you with meekness and fear." "By what authority doest thou these things?" is the focal point on which every religious issue turns. *Every religious issue is ultimately resolved on the principle of authority.*

Jesus responded to their question by asking them one: "The baptism of John, whence was it? from heaven, or of men?" Thus, Jesus clearly indicated that there are but two sources from which religious authority originates. It comes either from heaven or from earth, from God or from man. Every honest student knows, as they must have known, that John's baptism was divinely authorized. All who rejected John's baptism "rejected the counsel of God against themselves" (Luke 7:30). Luke affirmed that it came from heaven and not from men. Had these Jews admitted the truth in the matter, they would have stood self-condemned. They had but one answer: like so many professed religious leaders of our day, they simply could not or would not tell.

Every responsible person ought to know and be ready to "tell" the authority by which his religious life is directed. One's religion is no better than the authority upon which it rests. If John had not been a prophet of God, his preaching would have been worthless and his baptism vain. No man has

66

the right to legislate in religious matters. Any system of religion which is founded on human authority is empty, vain and powerless to save. Every tenet of the Christian's faith must stand "not in the wisdom of men, but in the power of God." Every faithful congregation of the Lord's people must be established, governed and maintained by a constant appeal to New Testament authority.

The power and authority of God has always resided in the word of God. In this gospel age, God executes His authority through His Son (Heb. 1:1-2). The Son has given the right to "bind and loose" the conditions of salvation to the apostles (Matt. 16:19). These apostles were given the Holy Spirit to guide them in revealing the will of God in the New Testament (John 16:13). The New Testament, therefore, represents the authority of God and of Christ. There is "none other to whom we can go." This means that any religious practice in which men engage, if it is not authorized by the New Testament, God did not authorize it, Jesus Christ did not command it, the apostles did not bind it, and the Holy Spirit has not revealed it to men.

CHART ON THE AUTHORITY OF REVELATION

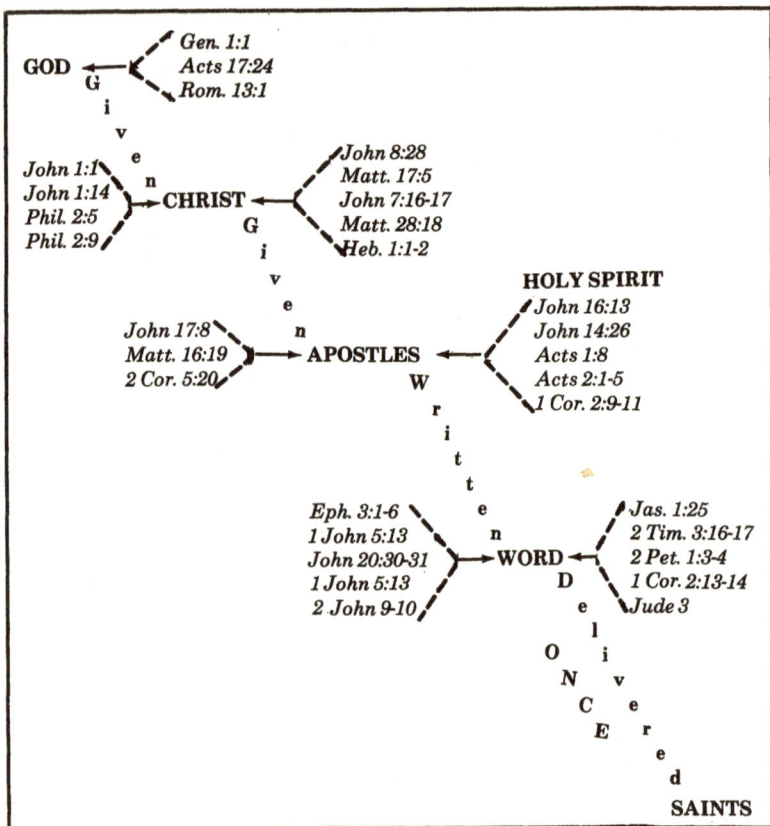

GOD ←
G
i
v
e
n

Gen. 1:1
Acts 17:24
Rom. 13:1

John 1:1
John 1:14
Phil. 2:5
Phil. 2:9
→ **CHRIST** ←
G
i
v
e
n

John 8:28
Matt. 17:5
John 7:16-17
Matt. 28:18
Heb. 1:1-2

HOLY SPIRIT

John 17:8
Matt. 16:19
2 Cor. 5:20
→ **APOSTLES** ←
W
r
i
t
t
e
n

John 16:13
John 14:26
Acts 1:8
Acts 2:1-5
1 Cor. 2:9-11

Eph. 3:1-6
1 John 5:13
John 20:30-31
1 John 5:13
2 John 9-10
→ **WORD** ←
D
e
l
i
v
e
r
e
d

Jas. 1:25
2 Tim. 3:16-17
2 Pet. 1:3-4
1 Cor. 2:13-14
Jude 3

O
N
C
E

SAINTS

Questions

1. All authority in the universe belongs to _____.
2. God gave His word to _____.
3. Jesus Christ gave His word to _____.
4. They were guided by the _____.
5. They have _____, and we can _____.
_____.
6. They were authorized by Jesus to _____ and _____.
7. The written word has been delivered to the_____.
8. It is _____, _____, _____ and _____.

CHAPTER V
Lesson I: The Church: The Kingdom Of Christ
Text

"To the intent that now unto the principalities and powers in heavenly places might be known by the church, the manifold wisdom of God, according to the eternal purpose which he purposed in Christ Jesus our Lord" (Eph. 3:10-11).

Commentary

According to this section of our original text, the church is the eternal purpose of God in Christ—the end result of God's purpose and plan for human redemption. It is a spiritual relationship between God and man wherein man can worship and serve the God of heaven in an acceptable manner. The text further states that the wisdom of God is known by the church. Just as a great work of art reflects the wisdom and skill of the artist who created it, so the church reflects the wisdom of God who planned it from eternity and brought it into existence by His Divine power.

It is important to note that the church and the kingdom are one and the same. They are simply different names for the same institution. There are many terms in both the Old and New Testaments which are used to identify this spiritual relationship between God and man, each setting forth a distinct feature of it. Although there are people who attempt to make a difference in the church and the kingdom, there is no scriptural basis for such a distinction. These people teach that the kingdom has not yet come, and that it will not be inaugurated until the second coming of the Lord. However, the New Testament clearly teaches that Christians in the first century were citizens in the kingdom. These same individuals are referred to as being members of the church. There are two historical lines of reference back to the Old Testament by which we can trace the development of the purpose of God with respect to the church:

A. The establishment of the Lord's House in the city of Jerusalem in the last days.

B. The inauguration of the kingdom and the coronation of the king on the throne of David in the days of the Roman kings. We shall study both of these references in the lessons which follow in this chapter.

Questions

Identity of the church and kingdom:

A. Matt. 16:18. Jesus promised to build His _____.

B. Matt. 16:19. He referred to it as the _____.

C. Col. 1:13. Members of the church had been translated into the _____.

D. Heb. 12:28. The Hebrew Christians were being received into the _____.

E. Rev. 1:9. John was a brother in the _____.

Other Terms Applied to the Christ:

A. John 15:1. Christ (the church) is called the _____.

B. John 15:6. Individual members are the _____.

C. Col. 1:18. The church is referred to as the _____.

B. 1 Tim. 3:15. The church is the _____.

C. Eph. 2:19. Ephesian Christians were God's _____.

Lesson II: The Church In Prophecy

Texts

Isa. 2:1-5; Mic. 4:1-5; Joel 2:28-32.

Commentary

I. *Establishment of the Church Prophecied:*

A. *Place*   *Jerusalem*

B. *Means*   *Texts*   *Teaching*

C. *Time*   *Last Days*

II. *Fulfilled in the New Testament:*

A. *Place: Jerusalem* (Luke 24:49, 52; Acts 2:1-5).

B. *Means: Teaching* (Acts 2:1-5; 2:22-26).

C. *Time: Last Days* (Acts 2:14-21).

III. *Prophetic Description of the Lord's House:*

A. *Universal in Scope:*

1. All nations would flow unto it.

2. Many people would go up to the mountain of the Lord.

B. *Exalted in Character:*

1. It would be exalted above the hills.

2. Established in the top of the mountain.

C. *Peaceful in Influence:*

1. God would judge between Jew and Gentile.

2. Swords would be made into plowshares and spears into pruning hooks.

3. Nation would not lift up sword against nation.

4. They would not learn war anymore.

D. *An Instructed Membership:*

1. The law of the Lord would be proclaimed.

2. God would teach them of His ways.

E. *An Obedient Membership:*

1. They would walk in His paths.

2. Thus, they would follow the instruction given to them from the word of the Lord.

IV. *New Testament Description Reveals The Same Qualities:*

    A. *The House Of God Identified As The Family of God.*

        1. The church of the living God (1 Tim. 3:15).

        2. It is the household of God (Eph. 2:19).

        3. The family which is named for Christ (Eph. 3:15).

        4. It is the household of faith.

    B. *The House of God Identified As the Temple of God.*

        1. It is God's holy temple (Eph. 2:21).

        2. It is a spiritual temple (1 Pet. 2:5).

        3. The Holy Spirit dwells in it (1 Cor. 3:16).

    C. *Universal in Scope:*

        1. The word of the Lord went forth from Jerusalem, beginning at Pentecost, and then to the uttermost parts of the earth (Luke 24:46-47; Acts 1:8; 2:1-47).

        2. The commission of Christ required a universal proclamation of the gospel (Matt. 28:19; Mark 16:15-16).

        3. It was preached to every creature under heaven (Col. 1:23).

    D. *Exalted in Character: Spiritual.*

        1. The church is a spiritual priesthood (1 Pet. 2:5).

        2. We are raised to sit in a heavenly place (Eph. 2:6-7).

        3. Affections to be set on things above (Col. 3:1-3).

    E. *A House of Peace* (Eph. 2:14-16).

        1. Christ is the peacemaker.

        2. God judged between Jew and Gentile by the gospel.

        3. Through His death, Christ removed the wall (the law) which separated them and, thus, made peace.

        4. Both Jew and Gentile were reconciled to God in one body, the church.

        5. The gospel was the means of reconciliation (2 Cor. 5:19).

    F. *An Instructed Membership:*

        1. Teaching was the means of bringing the church into existence on the day of Pentecost (Acts 2:22-47).

        2. Jesus required instruction in order for one to come to God (John 6:44-45).

3. The commission of Christ demands it (Matt. 28:18-20).

4. Freedom from sin requires knowledge (John 8:31-32).

G. *An Obedient Membership:*

1. It was so in the beginning of the church (Acts 2:41-47).

2. The saved were added to the church as a result of having received (obeyed) the word of the apostles.

3. It was true of the Gentiles at the house of Cornelius (Acts 10:47-48).

4. Christ saves the obedient (Heb. 5:8-9).

Concluding Note

Every case of conversion recorded in the Acts of the Apostles began with teaching and ended with obedience. Having thus obeyed, they experienced the spiritual birth and were added to the one body wherein they were reconciled to God.

Lesson III: The Church In Existence
Commentary

The church of Old Testament prophecy has its beginning on the first Pentecost after the resurrection of Christ. It was established in Jerusalem in A.D. 33. Having been formed under divine direction as the first congregation in history, it represented all that God designed the local church to be. It became, therefore, the inspired example for the local church in every succeeding generation. There is no indication in the New Testament that God would ever change His purpose and plan for the church; neither is there any indication that any man or group of men would ever be authorized to alter the divine arrangement.

When any group of people in any given locality desire to form a congregation of Christians, they must look to the church in Jerusalem as the God-given pattern. There are at least three reasons why this is true: (1) The events of Pentecost which resulted in the formation of the Church of Christ on earth took place under the guidance and direction of inspired men. (2) The description of that church as given in the book of Acts, was recorded by inspiration. It is, therefore, an infallible record. (3) The church in Jerusalem existed before any kind of false teaching had been introduced and before any departure from the faith had set in. It represents New Testament Christianity in its original purity and simplicity.

Some Characteristics

A. *United in Faith:*
    1. All of them obeyed the same commands (Acts 2:37-41).
    2. They continued in the apostles' doctrine (Acts 2:42).
    3. They were united in heart and soul (Acts 4:32).
B. Faithful in Worship:
    1. They were stedfast, dependable, faithful (Heb. 10:25).
    2. They continued in the essential items of worship (Acts 2:42).

C. *Zealous in Teaching:* Edification and Evangelism.

1. They taught daily, publicly and privately (Acts 5:42).

2. Stephen in Jerusalem (Acts 7).

3. They filled Jerusalem with their doctrine (Acts 5:28).

4. When they were driven from Jerusalem, they went everywhere preaching the word (Acts 8:4).

5. Philip in Samaria (Acts 8:5-12).

D. *Liberal in Giving of their Means:*

1. None claimed their possessions as theirs only (Acts 4:32).

2. Although there is no evidence that they were commanded to do so, they sold their possessions and shared them with others who were in need (Acts 4:34).

3. Distribution to those in need was made under the direction of the apostles (Acts 4:35).

E. *An Example of Local Benevolence:* Acts 6:1-6.

1. They recognized the problem and solved it.

2. Solved by the authority of the apostles.

3. Accomplished through the framework of the local church.

4. No other organization involved.

F. *God-Given Example of Discipline:* Acts 5:1-11.

1. The love of money — the first recorded sin in the church.

2. Ananias and Sapphira lied to God and to the Holy Spirit.

3. They were punished with physical death.

4. The lesson: sin in the church is not to be tolerated.

5. The result: the growth of the church (vs. 11, 14).

G. *They were happy as Christians* (Acts 2:46).

H. *They were respected in their community* (Acts 2:47).

I. *Jerusalem was a growing church* (Acts 2:47; 4:4).

Questions

1. How long was it after the resurrection of Christ before the church came into being? _____

2. What does the word *Pentecost* mean? _____

3. On what day of the week did it fall? _____

4. Name five things which Peter preached concerning Christ in vs. 22-36 of Acts 2: (a) _____
(b) _____ (c) _____ (d) _____
_____ (e) _____

5. Name the things connected with New Testament Christianity which had their beginnings on Pentecost:_____
_____
_____

6. What is "the gift of the Holy Spirit" of Acts 2:38? ____
_____

7. Explain Acts 2:39: _____
_____

Lesson IV: The Kingdom In Prophecy

Text

"And in the days of these kings shall the God of heaven set up a kingdom which shall never be destroyed; And the kingdom shall not be left to other people, but it shall break in pieces and consume all of these kingdoms, and it shall stand forever" (Dan. 2:44).

Commentary

The text states the conclusion drawn by the prophet in his interpretation of the dream of the king of Babylon while Daniel was a prisoner there. Daniel recalled the dream of Nebuchadnezzar and gave the meaning of it. The king had seen a great and terrible image with a head of gold, breast and arms of silver, belly and thighs of brass, legs of iron, feet part of iron and part of clay. He also saw a stone cut without hands which struck the image on its feet and broke it to pieces. The image was thus destroyed and carried away on the wind, but the stone became a great mountain which filled the whole earth (2:1-35).

According to Daniel's interpretation of the dream, the image represented four world kingdoms beginning with Babylon. They would and did arise in the historical order shown below:

> A. The head of gold. . . . . Babylon (v. 38)
> B. Breast and arms of silver . . . . . Medo-Persian Kingdom
> C. Belly and thighs of brass . . . . Macedonian Kingdom
> D. Legs and feet of iron and clay . . . . Roman Kingdom

Having made this interpretation, the prophet concluded by saying God would set up a kingdom "in the days of these kings." Since only one world kingdom can exist at any one point in time, "in the days of these kings" must have reference to the last kingdom named, Rome. The Roman kings were ruling when Jesus was born and were still in power when the kingdom of Christ was set up on the Pentecost of the second chapter of Acts.

As we have already suggested in Lesson I of this chapter,

77

the kingdom of Christ was in existence in the first century and Christ was enthroned as king when He ascended in the clouds to the Father. Since the kingdom was to endure forever, it follows that the kingdom is in existence now with Christ reigning upon the throne of David.

If the kingdom has not yet come, then the prophecies of the Old Testament respecting the kingdom were not fulfilled at the time God determined. Thus, He would have failed to keep His word and our confidence in His promises would be destroyed. Furthermore, Jesus made certain promises concerning the kingdom which He did not keep if the kingdom has not yet come. This would brand the Son of God as a liar and an imposter.

During His earthly ministry, Jesus declared that the kingdom of God was "at hand"—in the near future. He stated that it would come during the lifetime of the people of His generation (Mark 1:15; 1:9). Again, the New Testament writers affirmed that Christians in the first century were citizens in the kingdom.

Did the God who prophesied of the coming of the kingdom fail to fulfill those prophecies? Are the people of the generation of our Lord still living? Did the New Testament writers misrepresent the facts in the case? Could Christians be citizens in a kingdom which did not exist? What are the answers to these questions, if the kingdom has not been inaugurated?

Study the chart on the kingdom prophecies on the following page.

The Kingdom Prophecies Fulfilled

The Prophecies	The Fulfillment
Isa. 9:6-7— The Son would bear the government upon His shoulders. Ruling on the throne of David, He would order and establish His kingdom.	*Acts 2:25-36:* In his sermon on the day of Pentecost, Peter affirmed that these prophecies, along with Psa. 16, were fulfilled in resurrection and ascension of Jesus.
Luke 1:32— 2 Sam. 7:11-14— The Son would be given the throne of David.	
Dan. 7:13-14— The Son would come to the Ancient of Days in the clouds to receive His kingdom.	At the ascension of Jesus as the apostles watched, a cloud received Him out of their sight (Acts 1:9).
Mark 1:15— The time was fulfilled—the kingdom of God was near.	During the lifetime of Jesus on earth.
Mark 9:1— The kingdom would come during the lifetime of the people who lived during Jesus' earthly ministry.	If that promise has not been kept, those people are still living.
Zech. 6:13— Jesus, *The Branch*, would rule as king and priest at the same time.	If Jesus is not the king now, we have no high priest now. But we do have a high priest who is seated on the right hand of the throne of the majesty in the heavens (Heb. 8:1; 4:15; 7:24-28). Jesus could not be a priest on earth (Heb. 8:4). Therefore, He cannot be a king on earth.

Lesson V: The Kingdom In Existence
Introduction

That the coming of the kingdom of God on earth was a subject of Old Testament prophecy is evident from a study of the chart on the preceding page. It is also obvious that all of the Old Testament prophecies respecting the kingdom have been fulfilled. Isaiah prophecied that the Son would reign upon the throne of David and Peter affirmed on Pentecost that He had been raised to sit on David's throne as both Lord and Christ. Daniel said that the Son would come to the Father in the clouds to receive the kingdom and Luke said He did go to the Father in the clouds (Acts 1:9). Zechariah foretold the Branch who would reign as king and priest at the same time. The Hebrew writer declares that Jesus is priest now (Heb. 8:1-5; 7:24-28). If He is now priest, He is also king. Since there cannot be a king without a kingdom, the kingdom has already come.

New Testament References

A. Jesus announced the coming of the kingdom, saying that the time set by the prophets had been fulfilled (Mark 1:14-15).

B. He taught His disciples to pray for it. It had not come at that time (Matt. 6:9-10).

C. Joseph of Arimathea was waiting for the kingdom (Luke 23:50-51).

D. Jesus taught that the people of His generation would live to see the kingdom (Mark 9:1).

E. After the death and resurrection of Jesus, Philip preached things concerning the kingdom. This preaching was done after the kingdom had been established (Acts 8:5-12).

F. Paul preached the kingdom to the people of Rome (Acts 28:23).

G. In Heb. 12:23, Paul said that Christian Jews had come to the church; he said that these same Christians had received the kingdom (Heb. 12:28). The church and the kingdom are one.

How And When It Came
A. *The Promises of Christ Fulfilled:*

1. He said that it would come with power (Mark 9:1).

2. He promised the apostles that they would receive power when they were baptized in the Holy Spirit (Acts 1:5, 8).

3. He told them to go to Jerusalem and wait until they would be "endued with power from on high" (Luke 24:49).

4. They returned to Jerusalem and waited (Luke 24:52-53).

5. They were baptized in the Holy Spirit in Jerusalem on the day of Pentecost (Acts 2:1-5).

B. *Conclusion: The Kingdom Established:*

1. When the Spirit came, the power was given.

2. When the power came, the kingdom came into existence.

3. Therefore, the kingdom of God was inaugurated on earth on the first Pentecost after the resurrection of Christ.

Questions
1. Why was it necessary for the apostles to be baptized with the Holy Spirit?_____

2. Has anybody other than the apostles ever received the baptism of the Holy Spirit? _____ If yes, who?_____

3. Can people receive it today?_____ Why?_____

4. Can you now pray the prayer that Jesus taught His disciples to pray? _____ Explain: _____

5. When Philip preached things concerning the kingdom of God, what did he preach? _____

_____

Lesson VI: The King And The Kingdom

Text

"This Jesus hath God raised up, whereof we all are witnesses. Therefore being by the right hand of God exalted, and having received of the Father the promise of the Holy Ghost, he hath shed forth this which ye now see and hear. For David is not ascended into the heavens: but he saith himself, The Lord said unto my Lord, Sit thou on my right hand, until I make thy foes thy footstool. Therefore let all the house of Israel know assuredly, that God hath made that same Jesus, whom ye have crucified, both Lord and Christ" (Acts :32-36).

Commentary

In the study of the chart of Lesson V, it was observed that the prophets not only foretold the establishment of the kingdom, they also prophesied that authority in the kingdom would be given to the Son and that He would rule upon the throne of David. The prophet Isaiah promised the throne of David to the Son; the angel of God told the virgin Mary that Isaiah's promise would be fulfilled in her son (Isa. 9:6-7; Lk. 1:32-33). Nathan told David that God would raise up one of his seed to sit upon his throne. The writer of Hebrews identified that seed as Christ: "I will be to him a Father, and he shall be to me a Son" (2 Sam. 7:12-14; Heb. 1:5). In Psalms 2, David prophecied of the death of Jesus by the decree of Herod and Pilate but he declared that God would speak to them in His wrath: "Yet have I set my King upon my holy hill of Zion. I will declare the decree: The Lord hath said unto me, Thou art my Son; this day have I begotten thee." In Acts 13:33-34, Paul applied this prophecy to the resurrection of Christ. Thus by God's decree of Psalms 2 Jesus was seated upon the throne of David in heaven. The throne of David in the Old Testament was the throne of God. David simply occupied it by God's decree. The throne of David in the New Testament is God's throne, but Christ now sits upon it by reason of the authority delegated to Him by the Father (Matt. 28:18). The throne of David has been transferred from earth to heaven (Psa. 89:35-37). It is a spiritual throne in a spiritual kingdom.

Now to the text of this lesson. It is taken from the sermon

preached by Peter in the city of Jerusalem on the first Pentecost after the resurrection of Jesus. The text is the inspired interpretation of David's prophecy of the resurrection of Jesus as recorded in Psalms 16.

Peter explained that David was not speaking of himself, when he said, "For thou wilt not leave my soul in hell; neither wilt thou suffer thine Holy One to see corruption." David's body was still in the grave Peter said. The apostle applied Psalms 16 to the resurrection of Christ. David was a prophet of God, and he had knowledge of the promise of God "that of the fruit of his loins according to the flesh, he (God) would raise up Christ to sit on his (David's) throne."

Having thus explained the prophecy, Peter boldly affirmed that God had indeed raised His Son from the dead, and that Christ was now seated at God's right hand, exalted as both Lord and Christ. Therefore, all of the promises and prophecies of the coming king and kingdom were fulfilled in the resurrection and ascension of Jesus when He was seated upon the throne of David as described by Peter in the sermon preached by him on Pentecost. Those who heard and believed that preaching, having obeyed the command of verse 38, became the first citizens of the kingdom by the decree of the King.

The Authority of The King

I. That Jesus has been crowned King and exalted as the Head of the Church is evidenced by the following:

  A. *Acts 2:33-36:*

    1. He is exalted at _____.

    2. He has been made both _____ and _____.

    3. He is seated upon the throne of _____.

  B. *1 Peter 3:22:*

    1. He has gone into _____.

    2. He is at the _____.

    3. Angels, authorities and powers are _____.

  C. *Ephesians 1:20-23:*

    1. He is exalted above_____
_____.

    2. He is head over _____.

II. *The Reign of Christ* (1 Cor. 15:24-28).
  A. Is Jesus reigning now?_____
  B. How long will he reign? _____
  C. When and how will the end of His reign occur? _____

_____

  D. What is the one exception to the statement that God
has put all things under His feet? _____

  E. When the reign of Christ is ended, what position will
He then occupy?_____

_____

  F. Can Jesus ever have any more authority than He now
has? (Eph. 1:22-23)_____

_____

Lesson VII: The Nature Of The Kingdom

Commentary

For hundreds of years the Jews had looked for the advent of a Messiah, but they expected Him to establish a temporal, earthly kingdom like the nations around them. They looked for the time when the fleshly nation of Israel would be restored to all of her original glory and power. However, when Jesus made it clear that His kingdom was not to be of his world—a temporal, earthly one, they rejected Him and put Him to death; and in so doing helped in bringing to pass the eternal purpose of God (1 Cor. 2:6-8).

The apostle Peter affirmed that the Old Testament prophecies pointed to the salvation which is in Christ and that the events which they foretold had been fulfilled in the lives of Christians in the first century who had heard the gospel of Christ preached by "the Holy Ghost sent down from heaven." In Acts 26:7-23, Paul, while preaching to Agrippa, taught that the true hope of Israel as based upon these prophecies had been realized in the death and resurrection of Jesus. He further stated that in preaching the death and resurrection of Christ with the help of God, he was saying "none other things than those which the prophets and Moses did say should come."

Again the apostle Peter taught that in the resurrection of Christ and His entry into heaven, the authority which the Father had delegated to Him and the events embraced in the gospel dispensation happened in fulfillment of prophecies made by "all of the prophets from Samuel, and those that follow after." All of them had spoken of "these days," the days of the existence of the kingdom and the reign of the king (Acts 3:20-26).

Jesus told Pilate that His kingdom was not of this world. He further told him that His kingdom was not "from hence" (John 18). Jesus was simply saying that His kingdom was *here* or soon would be, but that it was not *from* here—it was not from earth, but from above. It was the kingdom of heaven on earth. It is not an earthly empire, it is a spiritual kingdom, and Christ is king.

The True Nature of the Kingdom

I. *Spiritual in Character:*

A. "My kingdom is not of this world" (John 18:36).

B. The kingdom is "within you" (Luke 17:20-21).

C. Consists of those who have been born again (John 3:1-8).

D. It is a kingdom of righteousness, peace and joy in the Holy Ghost (Rom. 14:17).

E. The ungodly have no part in it (Eph. 5:5).

II. *In Purpose: A Place of Service:*

A. We serve God acceptably in it (Heb. 12:28).

  1. In meekness.

  2. In godly fear.

B. The vineyard where Christians work (Matt. 20:1).

C. The kingdom where we worship God (Luke 22:29-30).

D. We glorify God in it (Eph. 3:21).

III. *Eternal in Duration:*

A. It will stand forever (Dan. 2:44).

B. It cannot be destroyed (Dan. 7:14).

C. An everlasting dominion (Luke 1:32).

D. The kingdom that cannot be moved (Heb. 12:28).

Whose Kingdom Is It?

A. Rom. 14:17 _____

B. John 18:36 _____

C. Matt. 12:41 _____

D. Col. 1:13-14 _____

E. Eph. 5:5 _____

F. Matt. 18:3 _____

G. Gal. 6:16 _____

How Do We Become Citizens In It?

A. Matt. 7:21 _____

B. John 3:1-5 _____

C. Matt. 18:3 _____

NOTE: Things equal to the same thing are equal to each other. Doing the Father's will equals entrance into the kingdom. Being born again equals entrance into the kingdom.

Becoming converted equals entrance into the kingdom. Therefore, doing God's will is the same as being born again, the same as being converted. They all mean the same thing.

1 Peter 1:22-23:

In the passage above, Peter summarized the whole matter of entrance into the kingdom as related to the steps above. He declared that Christians had been purified in obeying the truth and in so doing had been born again of incorruptible seed—the word of God. The new birth is simply obedience to the demands of the gospel of Christ.

Lesson VIII: The Future Of The Kingdom

Text

"For as in Adam all die, even so in Christ shall all be made alive. But every man in his own order; Christ, the firstfruits; afterward they that are Christ's, at his coming. Then cometh the end, when he shall have delivered up the kingdom to God, even the Father; when he shall have put down all rule and all authority and all power. For he must reign, till he hath put all enemies under his feet. The last enemy that shall be destroyed is death" (1 Cor. 15:22-26).

Introduction

The title of this lesson does not refer to the establishment of a kingdom sometime in the future but to the destiny of the kingdom of Christ already in existence. In this great chapter, Paul's great treatise on the resurrection, the apostle affirms (1) the resurrection of Christ as a proven historical fact, (2) a general resurrection of all of the dead as the result of His resurrection, (3) the inevitable consequences of disbelief in the resurrection, and (4) the universal resurrection as being the termination of the reign of Christ at which time He will "deliver up the kingdom to God, even the Father."

Note that the apostle does not refer to the "end" of the kingdom but to the end of the reign of Christ in His kingdom. When the "end," the universal resurrection, comes, He will deliver the kingdom to the Father. Jesus, having delivered the kingdom to the Father, will then "be subject unto him (the Father) that put all things under him, that God may be all in all" (v. 28). This will occur after "he hath put all enemies under his feet."

It should be noted here that there are two states of the kingdom set forth in the New Testament: (1) the present existence of the kingdom (the church) with Christ ruling on David's throne; (2) the future state in eternity—the church in heaven.

A. The Present Reign of Christ is Evidenced by:

1. Peter's declaration on Pentecost that Christ had been raised to "sit" on David's throne at God's right hand till all

foes are conquered (Acts 2:25-36). This statement fulfills the prophecies of 2 Sam. 7:12-14; Psa. 16; and Psa. 110:1.

2. The statement of the apostle to the Hebrews that Jesus, having "purged our sins," *sat* down on the right hand of the "Majesty on high." He then quoted the same prophecy quoted by Peter as a proof-text (Heb. 1:3, 13).

3. Finally, our text declares that He *must* reign till He has conquered the last enemy, death. The "sitting" and the "reigning" are identical and co-extensive. He must *sit,* and He *must* reign till "he hath put all enemies under his feet."

B. The Eternal State of the Kingdom is Evidenced by:

1. Paul's words in Acts 14:22. In this passage, Paul exhorted Christians to "continue in the faith," and assured them that "we must through much tribulation enter into the kingdom of God." The kingdom of God in this verse is Heaven, the home of all of God's faithful—the ultimate destiny of Christ's church.

2. Peter's affirmation that all who "make their calling and election sure" will be granted an abundant entrance into the "everlasting kingdom of our Lord and Saviour Jesus Christ" (2 Pet. 1:10-11).

3. It is evident, then, that all faithful citizens of the kingdom of Christ on earth will, "at his coming," be granted an eternal abode with God in Heaven, the ultimate destiny of the "kingdom of God's dear Son" (Col. 1:13).

4. However, let it be remembered that all of the un-faithful will be gathered out of His kingdom to receive a just recompense for their unfaithfulness (Matt. 13:41-42). This will take place "at his coming" at which time "the righteous shall shine forth as the sun in the kingdom of their Father" (v. 43).

Order of Events in the Text

A. The first thing mentioned is the resurrection of Christ.

B. Next, "they that are Christ's at his coming."

C. Then, "cometh the end." The word then connects the *end* with His *coming.* The second coming of Christ will be the *end,* not the *beginning* of His reign.

D. When the end comes, He (Christ) will deliver up the kingdom to the Father.

E. But the end will not come until the last enemy (death) has been destroyed.

F. Now the only means by which death can be destroyed is the universal resurrection of the dead. So long as one dead body remains in the grave, death is the victor. And so the apostle assured us in v. 54 that death shall be "swallowed up in victory." "But thanks be to God, which giveth us the victory through our Lord Jesus Christ" (v. 57). This victory over death was made possible by the death and resurrection of Christ. Such is the glorious hope of the faithful child of God.

The Teaching of Jesus Concerning the General Resurrection

A. All who have done good in this life, and all who have done evil will "come forth" from the grave in the same hour (Jn. 5:28-29). This passage makes no allowance for the premillennial view of a thousand year reign of Christ on earth between the resurrection of the righteous and the judgment of the wicked.

B. The individual who comes to Christ, having "heard and learned of the Father," will be raised up "at the last day" (Jn. 6:44-45). All who reject Christ by refusing to receive His Word will be judged by His Word "in the last day" (Jn. 12:48).

C. Both the "sheep" and the "goats" will be raised up to hear their sentence in the same day and hour (Matt. 25:31-46).

Concluding Observations

A. The *end* of our text *at His coming* will be:

1. The end of the material world (2 Pet. 3:7-10).

2. The end of man's preparation for judgment (2 Pet. 3:9; Heb. 9:27).

3. The time of the universal resurrection (Jn. 5:28-29; Jn. 6:40, 44-45).

4. The termination of the reign of Christ (text).

5. The judgment day (Jn. 12:48; 2 Thess. 1:5-10).

Questions

1. Why was it necessary for Paul to write concerning the resurrection in 1 Cor. 15? _____

_____

2. Explain the expression, "Christ the firstfruits." _____

_____

3. Who are "they that are Christ's at his coming"? _____

_____

4. God put all things in subjection to Christ with one exception. What is the exception? _____

_____

5. What will be the position of Christ when He has delivered up the kingdom to the Father? _____

_____

6. What passages prove that there can be no reign of one thousand years between the resurrection of the righteous and wicked?_____

_____

7. According to Peter, how does one make "his calling and election sure? _____

_____

8. What passage shows that the second coming of Christ will be an unexpected time? _____

_____

9. When will the "end" in our text take place? Give the passage. _____

10. How would you prove that death marks the end of man's period of preparation? _____

_____